Forbes BURNHAM
NATIONAL RECONCILIATION
AND NATIONAL UNITY 1984-1985

Forbes BURNHAM
NATIONAL RECONCILIATION AND NATIONAL UNITY 1984-1985

HALIM MAJEED

GLOBAL COMMUNICATIONS PUBLISHING
626 EAB PLAZA UNIONDALE, NEW YORK 11556

Copyright © Published by Global Communications Publishing

Published by Global Communications Publishing
626 EAB Plaza Uniondale, New York 11556

First Published 2005
© Global Communications Publishing
626 EAB Plaza Uniondale, New York 11556
ISBN 0-9772603-0-5

All rights reserved. No part of this publication may be
used or reproduced in any manner whatsoever without written
permission from the publisher, except in the case of
brief quotations embodied in critical articles and reviews.

Forbes Burnham
National Reconciliation And National Unity 1984-1985/Halim Majeed
Includes bibliographical references

Cover design & cover art © Lynn Franklin
Interior book design © Franklin & Franklin Graphics
Editor: Candice Rammesar
Printed in the United States

*DEDICATED TO MY WIFE, JENNY,
AND MY CHILDREN, DARREN AND ANEEDRA*

CONTENTS

	ACKNOWLEDGMENTS	x
	FOREWORD	xiv
	L.F.S BURNHAM: A BIOGRAPHICAL NOTE	1
	INTRODUCTION	19
1	THE OBJECTIVE AND SUBJECTIVE CONDITIONS OF POLITICAL DIALOGUE	29
2	PRELUDE TO DIALOGUE	39
3	THE START OF THE DIALOGUE PROCESS	55
4	THE POWER SHARING CONFIGURATION	61
5	THE END OF DIALOGUE	73
6	WHITHER GUYANA	89
	APPENDICIES	100
	NOTES	122
	BIBLIOGRAPHY	138

PREFACE

Forbes Burnham

ACKNOWLEDGMENTS

Several distinguished personalities have contributed in one way or another to make the publication of this book a reality. Space and other considerations have caused me to list only a few of them below.

I would like to express my sincere appreciation to Mr. Henry Skerret, former Editor-in Chief of the Kaieteur News, and Dr. Kenneth King, former Ambassador of Guyana to Brussels, for encouraging me to undertake the writing of this Book. They strongly believed that its contents were of great historical importance to the people of Guyana and that the book itself would be a significant addition to the current literature on contemporary Guyanese politics.

I would wish to acknowledge the valuable contribution of Mr. Robert Corbin, Leader of the People's National Congress, in providing me with background information and other details of the 1976 talks between the People's National Congress and the People's Progressive Party and for his other suggestions in the preparation of this publication.

I would like to recognize, with deep gratitude, the kind assistance that Mr. Ranji Chandisingh and Mr. Elvin McDavid have proffered to me in several ways to make this publication a reality. Individually and collectively, they supplemented my information and were at all times willing to clarify any issue about which I was uncertain. They have read the manuscript and have provided valuable advice in more ways than one. Without their inputs, I would have hardly considered the publication of this book.

I deeply value the comments of Dr. Perry Mars, the late Dr. Cedric Grant, Mr. Rashleigh Jackson, Mr. Malcolm Parris, Dr. Richard Van West Charles, Mr. Jeffrey Thomas, Mr. Donald Ainsworth, Mr. John Luard, and Ambassador Ronald Austin, among others, that have guided me in writing the book. They have provided useful perspectives in this undertaking and I thank them immensely for their assistance.

It would be remiss of me if I did not record my appreciation to the several members of the People's Progressive Party who have kindly consented to be interviewed by me and who, for understandable reasons, have requested that they remain anonymous at this time.

My good friend, Dr. Aubrey Bonnett, graciously agreed to write the Foreword to this book. We do not share an identity of political convictions but he believed that the contents of this publication have a certain political legitimacy that is required for historical rectification. I want to publicly thank him for his courage and forthrightness in writing the Foreword and for his suggestions and contributions toward the publication of this work.

I would like to thank my wife, Jenny, who has been patient with me in the preparation of this book and who has also given me tremendous support and encouragement to ensure that it is published.

And finally, I would like to thank my daughter, Aneedra, who has typed this entire book, for her infectious laughter - and without any single complaint.

Acknowledgments

Whatever flaws inhere in this publication are solely of my creation and I and I alone assume full responsibility for them.

Halim Majeed
New York
May 2005

FOREWORD

It was William Shakespeare who intoned that "the evil that men do lives after them; the good oft interred with their bones". This prophetic statement has a ring of verity for many statesmen: there is Richard Milhous Nixon, for example, who has been reviled as the President that was less than truthful to the people of the United States, who had committed an act that almost led to a traumatizing political impeachment before his ultimate resignation, who played the Cold War to his advantage and who, *inter alia*, engaged in profound red-baiting. Very little, however, is extolled about his focus on Black Capitalism; his efforts to enhance economic advancement for African Americans through the Philadelphia Plan; his rapprochement with China and his attempts to engage that "dormant" potential superpower whilst, at the same time, driving a political wedge between China and the USSR; his weakening of the Soviet Union's stranglehold on Eastern Europe and his subsequent contribution to the implosion of what President Ronald Regan described as the "evil empire".

And so it is with Linden Forbes Sampson Burnham – founder of the political party, the People's National Congress (PNC), and the first Executive President of the Cooperative Republic of Guyana.

For some, Forbes Burnham is perceived as an authoritarian leader whose socialist policies and programs brought ruin to Guyana's economy; one who was believed to be connected with the death of Guyanese historian and political leader of the Working People's Alliance (WPA), Dr. Walter Rodney; and one who was seen as intrinsic to the ethnic rivalries in the society between Indo-Guyanese and Afro-Guyanese. Others regard him as a disciplined nationalist whose fortitude and vision propelled Guyana to political independence; as a regional integrationist whose frame of reference and paradigmatic thrust contributed significantly to the formation and was a central actor in the formation of the Caribbean Community (CARICOM) and, indeed, other such ongoing successful Regional ventures; as a gifted and renowned orator and intellectual whose brilliance, pragmatic realism and leadership were able to attract the "best and brightest" to serve the Guyanese nation at crucial junctures in regional and world history.

In an earlier work, I described President Burnham as part of dual charismatic political formation that initially led to the rise of a popular movement in the 1950's, only to fall prey to the disintegrative forces of Guyana's plural society, and one who was not absolutely blameless of the factionalism that was rife between two national leaders. In fact, Mr. Burnham was a much more complex and nuanced historical figure – brilliant, visionary, cavalier, dashing and ensnaring; he could also be calculatingly determined, pragmatic and pointedly instrumental in the pursuit of his goals. And he was destined to play with the other great national leader – Dr. Cheddi Bharrat Jagan, General Secretary of the People's Progressive Party (PPP) – a lasting and tortuous role in the evolution of Guyana's history.

In this book we are fortunate to have a unique view and a distinctive frame to evaluate PNC Leader, Forbes Burnham, one written by a person who was privileged to work with him on an historical event, which if completed, would have been an integrative, transformative and centripetal force in this young, and now utterly fragmented nation – Guyana. Mr. Halim Majeed is in a prime position to provide insights into President Burnham as a nationalist and one dedicated to the profound unity of all of Guyana's peoples. He, along with another important functionary, Mr. Ranji Chandisingh, joined the PNC in 1976 and were given important leadership roles within that Party and the Government.

Mr. Majeed and Mr. Elvin McDavid were senior political advisers to President Forbes Burnham – almost akin to the roles that Mr. McGeorge Bundy and Mr. Arthur Schlesinger played for President John Kennedy, and which Mr. Karl Rove now performs for President George W. Bush. They were both the sounding board and, in some instances, the implementers and executors of political and other cognate action which could not emanate forcibly from the official organs of the State. Parenthetically, for example, we now know that just prior to his assassination President John Kennedy had authorized, and there were ongoing, high level backdoor discussions for a rapprochement with President Fidel Castro of Cuba.

So it was with Forbes Burnham, who Mr. Majeed tells us, had ordered and initiated high level discussions with Dr. Cheddi Jagan and the opposition PPP with regard to power sharing, in the hope that this process, if completed, would lead to true national reconciliation and organic unity among the two main contending ethnic groups and bring a modicum of peace and stability to his troubled land. This would have been an extraordinary event, if accomplished, for it would have set a fertile climate and conditions for vigorous development in the nation. But fortuitously and unfortunately Burnham, like Kennedy, died before it could have been accomplished, and his successor, in my view, neither had the inclination nor political gravitas to continue this formidable venture.

Halim Majeed takes us on a probing, lucid, and explanatory detour on the successes and obstacles that the Burnham Initiative engendered. He gives us insights into the machinations and inner working of key members of the PPP and the PNC who were less inclined to lend their support for this initiative, and adverts to some of the reasons for their hesitancy or outright impediments.

Key questions still remain. What were the real reasons that led President Desmond Hoyte, the new leader chosen previously by Mr. Burnham, to depart so radically from the Burnham Initiative? Were there any extrinsic involvements by the USA or the UK in Mr. Hoyte's decision? We must recall that Burnham had fallen into profound disfavor with President Regan and the country had suffered immensely for this. Were Hoyte's initial political and economic actions, his strivings to woo segments of the Indo– Guyanese population, and his apparent alienation of Mrs. Viola Burnham, the spouse of President Burnham, from the political mainstream all contextually driven by attempts to win favor with both extrinsic and intrinsic polities? To these and similar queries, Halim Majeed gives us his own explanatory schema in order to dissect and analyze some of these phenomena. I believe they are insightful and provide a unique window into the ongoing analysis of Guyana and its leadership.

Whither Guyana? Can Mr. Robert Corbin, the new PNC Leader, lead his Party to accomplish what President Burnham was unable to do – to form a Government of National Reconciliation? Would he be able to assist in neutralizing the influence of the old ideological dinosaur and matriarch of the PPP, Mrs. Janet Jagan, and emancipating President Bharat Jagdeo? Or is Guyana doomed to continued and increasing sectarian and political violence, worsening ethnic relations, social unrest, a crumbling infrastructure and an elite mired in the politics of survival and begotten to the "posses" of the criminal and drug underworld which at times find their services utilized by the political actors — all the classic characteristics of failed states ripe for regime change? Should a more innovative and aggressive form of Proportional Representation be utilized to maximize the governance process and build a more credible system of political legitimacy?

Years ago, noted sociologist and philosopher of science, Robert Merton, introduced the conceptual heuristic tool — insider/outsider perspectives as ways of analyzing social processes and organizations. The "insider", Merton contends, by virtue of his perspective can bring knowledge, ranging from monopolistic to privileged, to bear on the frames of analysis; with the "outsider," although not socialized within the group or organization, can bring a fresh, unbiased approach. Halim Majeed, in a sense, presents both perspectives — insider/outsider — in his analyses of these two political organizations, the PPP and PNC, and as such his insights are both refreshing and revealing.

This will, of course, not be the last word, the final answer; there will be other truth claims. However, this book will certainly stand as an important and substantive source in the ongoing political and theoretical debates and controversies surrounding Guyana, and its political past and future. Mr. Majeed has done a superb job and Caribbeanists and other diasporic scholars, practitioners, and most certainly the literate and sophisticated reader of events in developing societies would thoroughly enjoy reading this book. It is a sound and solid piece of work.

   Aubrey W. Bonnett, PhD
   Professor of American Studies, and
   Former Vice President of Academic Affairs,
   SUNY College at Old Westbury
   Dean Emeritus, College of Social Behavioral Sciences,
   California State University, San Bernardino
   Former Chairperson of Sociology at Hunter College, CUNY

May 2005

L.F.S BURNHAM – A BIOGRAPHICAL NOTE

"From the gay, witty and brilliant companion of years ago he has become the work-horse of the nation, demanding from his colleagues and himself prodigies of effort. I am not – and no man is – equipped to say what it is that a man should do with himself. Sacrifice is a personal decision.
—Martin Carter on L.F.S. Burnham (December 3, 1969)

His name is a household word in Guyana twenty years after his passing – for different reasons – and will be for a long time to come. His reputation as a leader and statesman is international and almost legendary. His capacity to grasp complex concepts was incredible. His courage to chart unknown waters was formidable. His brilliance was rare. When he died suddenly on August 6, 1985, Prime Minister Rajiv Gandhi of India referred to him as one of the outstanding leaders of the twentieth century.

Linden Forbes Sampson Burnham was born on February 20, 1923, in Kitty, Greater Georgetown, Guyana, and rose from humble beginnings to become one of the most extraordinary personalities in Guyana's history and politics, and indeed, the Caribbean and the Third World, in the last century. He was the second of two boys in a family of five siblings. His parents, James Ethelbert Burnham and Rachael Abigail Sampson, a progeny of Guyana's Amerindian peoples, were of the Methodist denomination. He attended the Kitty Methodist School where he acquired his primary education and, later, Central High School and Queen's College, Guyana's leading high school at that time, where he obtained his secondary education.

Mr. Burnham was remarkably brilliant, as the evidence has shown. He secured internal scholarships at Queen's College and, in 1942, at the age of nineteen; he was awarded the prized Guiana Scholarship which provided him with the opportunity of acquiring a university education in Great Britain. However, the vicissitudes of the Second World War prevented him, temporarily, from traveling to London but, in the meantime; he used the delay to complete his Bachelor's of Arts degree externally. Mr. Burnham taught briefly at his alma mater and among some of his students were Mr. Fred Wills[1], Sir Shridath Ramphal[2], Mr. Rashleigh Jackson[3], Mr. Bryn Pollard[4] and Mr. Keith Massiah[5]- all of whom later acquired impressive academic and professional distinctions and brought tremendous, enduring respect to Guyana.[6]

In 1945, Mr. Burnham went to London University where he received the LLB (Hons.) degree in 1947 and was called to the Bar at Gray's Inn the following year. In 1947 also, he was elected President of the West Indian Student' Union and led the West Indian Students' Delegation to the World Youth Festival in Prague.[7] It was during his student years that he became exposed to the writings of Karl Marx and subsequently identified both with the Communist Party of Great Britain and the left-wing London Branch of the Caribbean Labor Congress. He also became closely associated with the anti-colonial struggles and the anti-colonialist movements and endeared himself to his Caribbean and African colleagues.

His affiliation to the left-wing movement in the United Kingdom brought him in contact with the veteran Jamaican Marxist radical, William (Billy) Strachan, who urged him to return to Guyana and actively support the small anti-colonial group, the Political Affairs Committee, that had been started up by a young dentist, Dr. Cheddi Jagan[8], who had studied in the United States and had returned to Guyana in 1943.

But Mr. Burnham was not exactly a stranger to Dr. Jagan. Prior to his departure for London, he attended meetings at the Public Free Library, Georgetown, at which Dr. Jagan was usually present. For young Burnham, Dr. Jagan represented a revolutionary icon at the time.

Mr. Burnham remigrated to Guyana in 1949, joining forces with Dr. Jagan and, in 1950, co-founded the People's Progressive Party (PPP), named by him, and became its first Chairman. The nationalist movement in Guyana was born. Actually, in the embryonic process of Party formation it was understood that Mr. Burnham would have been designated the Party Leader and so it appeared strange to him when Dr. Jagan's influence in the Party did not seem to prevail. At that time also, it was considered that the Party should have co-leaders, similar to the leadership structure of the Working People's Alliance (WPA)[9], given the ethnic realities of the country.

In 1951, Mr. Burnham married Ms. Sheila Bernice Lataste, a Trinidadian optometrist, and the union produced three children, Roxanne, Annabelle and Francesca. A few years later, they went their separate ways.

Meanwhile, Mr. Burnham had won the respect of, and a following in, the trade union movement. In 1952, he was elected President of the British Guiana Labour Union (later the Guyana Labour Union) and held the Presidency until his death. He played a sterling role in that connection and was a positive influence on other trade unions. As Dr. Jagan himself pointed out, with Mr. Burnham leading the British Guiana Labour Union "...increasingly the unions representing government employees came under militant, progressive leadership. As a result by 1953, British Guiana had a militant and dynamic Trades Union Council working closely with us."[10] At the same time, he found time to involve himself in community activities and in 1950-51, he served as President of the Kitty Brotherhood Movement.

By 1953, the People's Progressive Party "was forged into a strong political body ready to fight a general election under a constitution which allowed for the first time adult suffrage at the age of 21."[11] When the PPP triumphed at the elections that year, Mr. Burnham was appointed the country's first Minister of Education.

The newly elected PPP government of 1953 lasted 133 days in office. The British suspended the Constitution and imposed an interim government. One of the responses of the PPP leadership was to authorize both Mr. Burnham and Dr. Jagan to travel to Great Britain and India, among other countries, to mobilize public opinion against the British ouster of the PPP Government. But even during this time of active colonial oppression, the PPP leadership did not respond as a united, monolithic group. Disagreements on tactics, the Party's political line, and the issue of leadership under new circumstances, among other things, gave way, finally, to manifest fragmentation.

It was not surprising, therefore, that Mr. Burnham left from the PPP in 1955 – for personal and ideological reasons – and not on the basis of "opportunistic" or "racist" grounds, as some of his erstwhile colleagues are wont to argue. He criticized the Party's intolerance of dissenting points of view (which, it would appear, continues to be evidenced in this modern epoch by the expulsion of PPP Central Committee Member, Mr. Khemraj Ramjattan) arguing that openness must be the hallmark of internal political debates.[12] He disagreed with the PPP's "adventurist policies" at the time in dealing with the British Government, submitting that socialism cannot be built in a colony. It was his firm conviction that the country must first achieve political independence and then pursue its socialist goals.

Mr. Burnham came to the conclusion that Dr. Jagan was neither a perspicacious nor pragmatic leader, who could deal with the national political situation and the internal dynamics of the PPP at the time, given the aggressive nature of British colonialism and the vagaries of the Cold War. He, therefore, walked away from the PPP under the leadership of Dr. Cheddi Jagan and Mrs. Janet Jagan[13], accompanied by Indo-Guyanese political stalwarts such as Mr. J.P. Lachmansingh and Mr. Jainarine Singh. The repeated notion that the British "engineered" the "split" in the PPP leadership is fallacious and has nothing to do with reality but everything with myth making. Indeed, shortly afterwards, a group of other Party stalwarts, Mr. Martin Carter, Mr. Rory Westmaas, Mr. Lionel Jeffrey, and Mr. Keith Carter also left the PPP. That trend of migration continued until in the 1990's.

For a time, Mr. Burnham headed the People's Progressive Party (Burnhamite), and then decided that his movement needed a new name and a fresh character. Thus, in 1957, the People's National Congress (PNC) came into being and Mr. Burnham was elected its first leader. Two distinguished Indo-Guyanese political figures, Mr. J.P Lachmansingh and Mr. Jainarine Singh, were also elected Chairman and General Secretary respectively.

Yet, despite his hectic career as a politician and trade unionist, he earned the reputation as one of the Guyana's leading attorneys. His advocacy at the bar, his superb eloquence, and his mastery of the law placed him, perhaps *primus inter pares*, with the legal luminaries of his time. It was, therefore, not surprising that in 1959, he was elected President of the British Guiana Bar Association and, in 1960, appointed a Queen's Counsel.

The period, 1957-64, saw Mr. Burnham strenuously engaged in party building and forming political alliances. Under his leadership, the PNC acquired new offices and, slowly but certainly, the new party machinery was put in place. During this time also, the Women's Auxiliary of the PNC and the PNC Youth Organization were launched to buttress the Party's political work. In terms of political tactics, he coalesced with the United Democratic Party (UDP)[14] and fought the 1961 General Elections increasing his voting strength in the Legislative Assembly from three seats in 1957 to eleven. At the same time during 1959-1964, Mr. Burnham served as Mayor of Georgetown.

Mr. Burnham and the PNC lost the 1961 elections but not the will to survive and surmount. Indeed, in the immediate aftermath of the 1964 General Elections, fought under Proportional Representation, the PNC combined with the United Force (UF)[15] to form the PNC-UF Coalition Government, garnering 53 per cent of the popular vote with the PPP gaining 46 per cent. The tactic of political coalition between the PNC and the UF ended the PPP's governmental dominance of seven years - even as the PPP leadership proclaimed that it was "cheated not defeated" at the polls[16].

The assumption of Mr. Burnham to the Prime Ministership of British Guiana in December 1964 opened a new chapter in the history of the colony. Striving assiduously but firmly to usher in a regime of peace, stability and economic buoyancy, he immediately began to set his sights on gaining political independence as quickly as possible. Some seventeen months later, on May 26, 1966, Great Britain granted the colony of British Guiana full independence. It was an emotional moment with Mr. Burnham and Dr. Jagan embracing each other as the Golden Arrowhead, the new national flag, was unfurled by young army Lieutenant Desmond Roberts (later to become the Director-General of the Guyana National Service) to signal the birth of the new independent Guyana. Later, Dr. Jagan characterized national independence as "the stage of neocolonialism which Guyana has now embarked upon."[17]

In 1967, Mr. Burnham walked down the aisle again, this time with Ms. Viola Victorine Harper, a highly qualified schoolmistress at Bishop's High School. That marriage brought forth two children, Melanie and Ulele.

For Prime Minister Burnham, political independence was just the first step to true nationhood. He, therefore, articulated the belief that the next objective should be the attainment of Republicanism. In proposing the Motion in the National Assembly to declare Guyana a Republic, he observed that "moving to the status of a republic represents, to my mind, a further step in the direction of self-reliance and self-confidence…we have decided that the monarchy should go."[18] Indeed, he saw Republicanism "as cutting us loose from a syndrome of dependency – political, economic, cultural, and psychological."[19] His concern was "to bolster our sense of self-worth and foster a nationalistic fervor that would make us confident in our ability and capacity to work at a level of sustained excellence, to convert our country into a modern, developed, prosperous State."[20]

Republicanism was one of the very few issues on which the PNC and the PPP were unanimously agreed. As a matter of fact, in 1969, it was Dr. Jagan who had urged the Government to declare February 23 a national holiday to mark the historical episode of the 1763 Berbice Slave Revolt, which was spearheaded by the enslave African, Cuffy (Kofi). He went on to advance the argument that that holiday "should be treated as a national event, and not made to appear as if it held particular significance for any one race group in Guyana."[21] The following year, the country acceded to Republican status.

By that time, under Prime Minister Burnham's leadership, new institutions were being developed and massive infrastructural developments had taken place, the Guyana Defence Force was established, the National Insurance Scheme was introduced, the construction of new multilateral schools[22] and Teachers' Training Colleges had begun and the University of Guyana had moved from the Queen's College Compound in Georgetown to the new sprawling Turkeyen Campus on the East Coast of Demerara. Tremendous infrastructural works in the areas of pure water supply, sea defense, drainage and irrigation, and electricity generation were being undertaken. The Black Bush and Tapakuma agricultural schemes were completed and the new international airport was opened.[23]

Mr. Burnham gave special recognition to Guyana's religious, ethnic and cultural diversity. His Government declared the Muslim festivals of Eid-Ul-Azaha and Youman Nabi, and the Hindu celebrations of Phagwah and Deepavali, national holidays under the Public Holidays (Amendment) Act approved by the National Assembly in 1967. Subsequently, Guyana's international airport was renamed "Timehri" as a mark of national respect, honor and acknowledgement of the contributions of Guyana's indigenous peoples, the Amerindians, to the nation's history and heritage[24]. During this time, Mr. Burnham introduced the philosophy and practice of self-help and self-reliance and this resulted in many productive enterprises. It was, indeed, a period of great ferment and activity in the country.

In the decade, 1970-1980, Prime Minister Burnham spearheaded a number of far reaching changes in the emergent nation-state. Consistent with its policy of ownership and control of the country's natural resources, the People's National Congress Government nationalized the Demerara Bauxite Company in 1970 with the full support of the People's Progressive Party. Later on, Reynolds Metal Company, and the sugar industry, owned by Bookers and Jessels, were nationalized, again with the complete backing of PPP, as were the Royal Bank of Canada, Barclays International, and the Chase Manhattan Bank. During this period, the Burnham-led Government acquired several other foreign companies.

On the socio-cultural front, Mr. Burnham's Government introduced free education from kindergarten to university in 1976, again with the full support of the PPP, and the Guyana Festival of Arts, introduced one year before, the logical successor to the Caribbean Festival of Arts (CARIFESTA), became an annual event in the country's cultural calendar. In 1979, Nrityageet, an aesthetic and colorful representation of East Indian dances, songs and drama, organized by the famous Shah Sisters, Nadira and Indranie, was launched at the National Cultural Center. In 2004, Nrityageet celebrated twenty-five years of its existence.

During this period, too, there was a substantial expansion of programs at the University of Guyana and, at the same time, training of Guyanese abroad, particularly in socialist countries, was intensified. At this time also, the National Science and Research Council, headed by the illustrious Dr. Pat Munroe, was established.

In terms of women's development, the People's National Congress Government launched the Committee on the Affairs and Status of Women in 1972, which was headed by

Mrs. Viola Burnham, Chairman of the Women's Revolutionary Socialist Movement (WRSM), the women's arm of the People's National Congress, with the aim of promoting the economic, educational, social and cultural advancement of women in Guyana. Four years later, the State Paper on the Equality of Women was presented and adopted in the National Assembly. That document laid the basis for removing a wide range of hitherto discriminatory measures against women.

Ever since he acceded to the Office of the Prime Minister, Mr. Burnham placed special emphasis on the well-being of Guyana's indigenous peoples. In 1976, after three years of intensive consultations, Prime Minister Burnham caused land titles to be vested in Amerindian communities. By the Amerindian (Amendment) Act, piloted in the National Assembly by Mr. Hugh Desmond Hoyte, then Minister of Economic Development, Amerindians had become proud inheritors of ancestral lands, legal ownership of which had eluded them for generations.

At the regional level, Mr. Burnham played a preponderant role in pursuing his vision of Caribbean integration. With the active support of two other Caribbean giants, Mr. Vere Bird of Antigua and Barbuda, and Mr. Errol Barrow of Barbados, he pioneered the Caribbean Free Trade Association (CARIFTA), the forerunner of the Caribbean Community (CARICOM).

Prime Minister Burnham was one of the original signatories to the 1973 Treaty of Chaguaramas, which brought the Caribbean Community and Common Market into being[25]. A year earlier, in 1972, in a bold, courageous and independent act of sovereignty Mr. Burnham led the way for the establishment of diplomatic relations with Cuba. He was able by his sheer statesmanship to bring on board Prime

Ministers Michael Manley of Jamaica, Errol Barrow of Barbados and Eric Williams of Trinidad and Tobago in this effort to restore Cuba to its rightful place in the Caribbean regional fraternity. Indeed, he was regarded as the de facto regional advocate and leader.

And so in 1979, when Mr. Maurice Bishop of Grenada assumed the reins of Government by extra-parliamentary methods, among the very first Heads of Government that he contacted for advice and support was Prime Minister Burnham.[26] In fact, shortly afterwards, Mr. Kester Alves, then Political Assistant to Prime Minister Burnham, now deceased, was instructed to travel to Grenada to obtain first hand information on the situation. On his return to Guyana, he was accompanied by two leading representatives of Mr. Bishop's New Jewel Movement, Mr. Unison Whiteman and Mr. Selwyn Strachan, whose purpose was to fully brief Mr. Burnham on the unfolding political developments in that CARICOM Member State.

At the wider international level, Mr. Burnham led the Caribbean in opposing apartheid in South Africa and became a formidable ally of the liberation movements of Africa. Moving from rhetoric to reality, he provided financial support to those movements, having received parliamentary approval to proceed in that manner. In 1970, Guyana became a formal member of the Non-Aligned Movement[27] and participated in the Lusaka Summit with Prime Minister Burnham leading the Guyana Delegation. After that event, in a show of solidarity with Africa, he visited Zambia, Uganda, Kenya, Tanzania and Ethiopia.

Mr. Burnham's high profile on the international arena impacted favorably on Guyana's image abroad. In 1974, the country was elected to the non-permanent membership of the UN Security Council. It was to repeat that sterling achievement in 1983. In that same year, 1974, Mr. Rashleigh Jackson, then Guyana's Permanent Representative to the United Nations and later Minister of Foreign Affairs, was elected to the Presidency of the United Nations Council for Namibia, and in 1975-76, represented Guyana on the UN Security Council. During that period, Mr. Denis Benn, former Head of the Economic Division in the Ministry of Foreign Affairs, was appointed Guyana's principal representative on the UNDP Governing Council and Sir Shridath Ramphal, former Attorney General and Minister of Foreign Affairs, was elected Secretary-General of the Commonwealth.

That pattern continued as other highly qualified Guyanese took their places on the international scene. Mr. Noel Sinclair, former Director-General in the Ministry of Foreign Affairs and Guyana's Permanent Representative at the United Nations, was appointed Deputy Secretary-General of SELA[28]. Later, Dr. Mohammed Shahabuddin, former Attorney General and Deputy Prime Minister, was elected to the World Court in The Hague, and Mr. Carl Greenidge, former Minister of Finance, was elected Deputy Secretary-General of the ACP Group of countries.[29]

As his philosophy of socialism became more manifest, Mr. Burnham began developing closer links with the world socialist community. Relations were being forged at both the levels of the Party and the State. He visited the Soviet Union, the People's Republic of China, Bulgaria, Cuba and Yugoslavia, among other communist countries. He developed a warm and trusted friendship with Prime Minister Indira Gandhi of India and Prime Minister Bandaranaike of Sri Lanka and, at the same time, was a confidant of President Fidel Castro of Cuba, President Julius Nyerere of Tanzania, President Kenneth Kaunda of Zambia, Prime Minister Errol

Barrow of Barbados, and Prime Minister Michael Manley of Jamaica.

By this time, Prime Minister Burnham's domestic policies, his international positions and, indeed, his world outlook were perceived by the United States Administration as being inconsistent with US interests, and that perception created serious tensions for Guyana-United States bilateral relations. It reached a head when, on October 6, 1976, anti-Castro terrorists, Orlando Bosch, Luis Posada Carriles and their collaborators, masterminded the bombing of a Cuban aircraft off the coast of Barbados.[30] CU 144, which was carrying a number of Guyanese students to Cuba for professional training, exploded in mid-air killing all on board, including Cubans and North Koreans. This unease in relations was to be repeated in 1983 when the United States invaded Grenada, subsequent to the execution of Prime Minister Maurice Bishop in the aftermath of the implosion of the Grenadian socialist experiment.[31]

In 1977, under Prime Minister Burnham's leadership, Guyana made a formal application for membership in the Council for Mutual Economic Assistance (CMEA)[32] and this move was again supported by the PPP. The Prime Minister's initiative was consistent with his perception of linking Guyana's economy with centrally-planned economies of the world socialist system.

Consequent on the promulgation of a new Constitution of Guyana in 1980, Mr. Burnham became Executive President and Head of State. It was during this period that he had to deal with three major issues all of which were adversely affecting the already fragile economic situation and, therefore, the quality of life of citizens: firstly, the harsh global economic conditions, which played a significant role in the deterioration of the national economy; secondly, economic and political pressure, including a substantial reduction of aid programs, from the western nations and the multilateral financial institutions, and, thirdly, the persistent undermining of the national economy by the PPP through its trade union arm, the Guyana Agricultural and General Workers Union (GAWU). In the latter regard, World Bank documents have indicated that between 1980-1985, there were 4,229 strikes in the sugar industry alone, with thousands of acres of cane destroyed through arson.[33]

Those pressures did not completely halt development. In 1980, under President Burnham's Administration, the Institute of Applied Science and Technology was established, and between 1980 and 1982, some thirty-five schools were constructed. In 1984, the National Agricultural Research Institute (NARI) came into being and shortly before Mr. Burnham died, President's College, a School of Excellence, his brainchild, had already assumed form.

But, at the personal level, Mr. Burnham's titanic struggle with the International Monetary Fund (IMF) in the period 1978-1985, the opposition that he encountered from the Inter-American Development Bank, and the unrelenting pressure generated by the Venezuelan border controversy greatly sapped his energy and had begun to quietly take a toll on his health. He had viewed the IMF as an unrestrained tool of imperialism trying to dismantle the socialist state which he was pioneering and it would seem that he had taken on that difficulty more personally than politically.[34] At the same time, he was also terribly disappointed by the reality that the USSR and the other Eastern European socialist countries were not more forthcoming and generous with their trade and economic programs.

President Burnham was the recipient of many honors and awards including the Order of Excellence (Guyana), the

Jose Marti Award (Cuba), and the Stara Planina Order (Bulgaria). He also received honors from Yugoslavia, Zimbabwe, Zambia, Tanzania, and the People's Republic of China, among other countries.

Sometimes, particularly his political opponents would ask: what legacy did President Burnham leave behind? Mr. Hugh Desmond Hoyte, the lately deceased Leader of the People's National Congress and former President of Guyana, summed it up very aptly.

"He brought us the blessings of peace, which we have enjoyed for over twenty years.

"He won for us our political independence.

"He preserved that independence and our territorial integrity in the face of great difficulties.

"He brought the strategic sectors of the Guyanese economy into the ownership and control of the Guyanese people.

"He transformed us from a motley collection of people into a truly Guyanese nation with clear objectives, a firm purpose and a common destiny.

"He developed in us a sense of self-reliance.

"He taught us to assert and defend our dignity, and inculcated in us respect for our fellow citizens, for our culture and for our heritage.

"He destroyed the bastions of prejudice, vested interests, discrimination and other forms of social injustice in our country and created equal opportunities for all citizens to develop their talents fully; and to this end, he introduced free education from nursery to university.

"He brought us small as we are, out of obscurity and made us known, respected and admired internationally – in the Non-aligned

Movement, in the Third World generally and in the councils of the United Nations.

"He dedicated himself to the ideal of regional integration and was the driving force in the processes which culminated in the establishment of the Caribbean Community.

"He laid, well and truly, the foundation for the development of a stable, productive, humane and prosperous society...

"Comrade Burnham found us divided; he left us a united people. He found us at war among ourselves; he left us at peace. He found us colonials; he left us proud, independent Guyanese; He found us uncertain of ourselves; he left us self-confident. He found us directionless; he left us with a clear purpose to enlarge and defend our freedom, our dignity, and our self-respect. He found us with meager economic ambitions; he left us with the bright prospect of prosperity. He found us with our eyes downcast; he taught us to aim for the stars."[35]

President Burnham's achievements will certainly withstand the test of any scrutiny. They were secured in the midst of external aggression and destabilization, and internal turmoil. Territorial threats came from the eastern and western fronts; the purveyors of the old order campaigned strenuously to halt the march of national development, and the political opposition at home played havoc with the foundations of the national economy. It is little wonder, therefore, that in an online poll conducted a few years ago in the Region he was declared "Caribbean Man of the Century."

New historians and historiographers, as separate and distinct from myth-makers, poison-pen scribblers and charlatans, will one day objectively examine his contributions to national, regional and international developments and record his successes – and his shortcomings. For, after all, he was human. But his place in history is secure and future generations of Guyanese will one day study him from a qualitatively different standpoint – as the formidable intellectual, resolute leader and shrewd statesman that he was.

Lord Tennyson's excerpted lines below capture, to my mind, some dimensions of the life and times of President Burnham whose name, I believe, will endure for many generations to come.

> ...I will drink
> Life to the lees: all times I have enjoy'd
> Greatly, have suffer'd greatly, both with those
> That loved me, and alone; on shore, and when
> Thro' scudding drifts the rainy Hyades
> Vext the dim sea. I am become a name;
> For always roaming with a hungry heart
> Much have I seen and known; cities of men
> And manners, climates, councils, governments,
> Myself not least, but honour'd of them all:
> And drunk delight of battle with my peers,
> Far on the ringing plains of windy Troy.
> I am a part of all that I have met;
>
> Yet all experience is an arch wherethro'
> Gleams that untravell'd world whose margin fades
> For ever and for ever when I move.
> How dull it is to pause, to make an end,
> To rust unburnish'd, not to shine in use!

Forbes Burnham

As tho' to breathe were life!

Death closes all: but something ere the end,
Some work of noble note, may yet be done,
Not unbecoming men that strove with gods.
The light begins to twinkle from the rocks;
The long day wanes; the slow moon climbs; the deep
Moans round with many voices. Come, my friends.
'Tis not too late to seek a newer world.
Push off, and sitting well in order smite
The sounding furrows; for my purpose holds
To sail beyond the sunset, and the baths
Of all western stars, until I die.
It may be that the gulfs will wash us down;
It may be we shall touch the Happy Isles,
And see the great Achilles, whom we knew.
Tho' much is taken, much abides; and tho'
We are not now that strength which in old days
Moved earth and heaven, that which we are, we are,
One equal temper of heroic hearts,
Made weak by time and fate, but strong in will
To strive, to seek, to find, and not to yield.[36]

INTRODUCTION

Early 1999, I wrote a three-part series in the Kaieteur News titled, Political Dialogue and Power Sharing: The 1984-85 Burnham Initiative. It attracted national attention.[37] For the first time, the veil of secrecy was lifted from this historical event in which the People's National Congress and the People's Progressive Party were involved and the range of issues brought to public knowledge.

The events described herein are not hearsay. They constitute an authentic and authoritative narrative in which the author played a facilitating and operational role. In addition, the full text of this book was reviewed by most of the leading players who participated in that landmark political episode in Guyana's history in order to confirm its accuracy.

The initial idea of developing the three articles into a comprehensive publication came from two friends, Mr. Henry Skerret, a former Editor-in-Chief of the Kaieteur News, and Dr. Kenneth King, who was until recently, Guyana's Ambassador to Brussels. Subsequently, Mr. Elvin McDavid, Chief Political Adviser to President Burnham, and Mr. Ranji Chandisingh, former Vice-President and Deputy Prime Minister, among others, played an important, if not catalytic, role in providing additional background information and verifying the sequence of events as they unfolded. The analyses and any subjective interpretation of the facts as I understand them are solely mine and I take full responsibility for whatever shortcomings may reside in them.

The fundamental reason for bringing the Burnham Initiative into the public domain is to give another perspective of the evolution of Guyana's political process, in general, and to demonstrate a different dimension of President L.F.S. Burnham's approach to the issues of national governance, political cohesion and national unity. For far too long, more of the positive aspects of his tenure in Government have remained hidden in the maelstrom of ideological subterfuges or distorted by political animus. Twenty years after his death is time enough that his efforts to genuinely effectuate political harmony with the People's Progressive Party and to build a unified Guyanese nation be known to current and future generations.

For it is still common in some circles to deny that President Burnham was interested in national unity and to depict him as a "racist" - using Arthur Schlesinger's emotive and highly prejudiced description (which he ascribed to the British) as gospel.[38] Indeed, some still continue to describe President Burnham's Administration as 'fascist' and 'dictatorship' knowing full well that those characterizations are absolutely incorrect as applied to the Guyanese context. The paradox, which inheres in this situation, is that although the People's Progressive Party used those appellations from time to time to describe the People's National Congress, it held formal discussions with the 'dictatorship' on two occasions, in 1976 and in 1984, in an effort to form a national front government and, indeed, demonstrated an active interest in political partnership with the People's National Congress.

Ever since the publication of *The Declaration of Sophia* in 1974,[39] widely regarded as one of the earliest public affirmations of the People's National Congress' anti-imperialist position, many influential members of the leadership of the

People's Progressive Party began to seriously analyze that new development in a scientific, objective manner. That, together with other developments taken by the People's National Congress quietly initiated a movement within the PPP's hierarchy to re-assess the political and ideological directions of the ruling party.

With Guyana's accession to Republican status, the nationalization of the bauxite industry, the establishment of diplomatic relations with the USSR, China and Cuba, and other socialist countries, and the linkages with the Non-Aligned Movement and the World Socialist Community, among other things, the PPP's oft-advanced argument that the People's National Congress was operating under the dictates of imperialism was no longer tenable. It could, therefore, no more continue to append the pro-imperialist label to the People's National Congress with any degree of legitimacy or credibility. Indeed, it began to venture into the realm of ideological technicalities in vogue at the time to demonstrate that the PNC was indeed a creature of imperialism.

But the political antagonisms were deep-rooted, especially in the minds of those in the PPP leadership whose differences were underlined by bitter personal animosities. A thoroughly objective analysis, therefore, of the political developments in Guyana by the Party's leadership, as a whole, was difficult. However, the 1975 Meeting of Latin American Communist Parties held in Havana, Cuba, which was attended by PPP General Secretary, Dr. Cheddi Jagan, greatly facilitated a political re-assessment of Guyana's political environment.[40] In this connection, the role of the highly respected General Secretary of the Communist Party of Uruguay, Rodney Arismendi, Vice President of Cuba, Carlos

Rafael Rodriguez, and other high-level members of the Political Bureau of the Communist Party of Cuba (CPC), in persuading Dr. Jagan that the PPP must adopt a realistic position vis-à-vis the PNC or be "left out in the cold" must be acknowledged and made public.[41]

On his return from Cuba, Dr. Jagan declared a new political approach in dealing with the People's National Congress Government. He stated that the PPP's political line would shift from non-cooperation and civil resistance to one of "critical support." In enunciating this new policy position, he declared that the possibilities now existed for a real breakthrough in Guyana and of rapidly moving to anti-imperialism and socialism and that conditions were perhaps better here than in any other country in Asia, Africa and Latin America. Guyana, the PPP General Secretary stated, had the possibilities of truly becoming a second Cuba.[42]

Dr. Jagan, subsequently, pointed out that the People's National Congress had put socialism on the agenda for Guyana and that the PPP could not close its eyes to the changes brought about by the PNC Government. He reiterated that "our political line should be changed from non-cooperation and civil resistance to critical support. This can lay the basis for a political solution."[43] He then went on to point out that if the reactionary forces succeeded in their endeavors and the PNC government was overthrown, "our heads will first roll."[44]

The following year, in 1976 the PNC Leader took the bold step of quietly attempting to forge a coalition with the PPP. The Communist Party of Cuba played a significant part in this affair. In fact, Mr. Burnham directed that this undertaking with the People's Progressive Party be initiated in Cuba on the occasion of the First Congress of the CPC, which was attended by Messrs. Hubert Jack, Steve Narine and Elvin McDavid representing the People's National Congress. Mr. Jack was designated spokesperson for the PNC on this development and piloted the initiative on the directions of Mr. Burnham. Later that year, the Head of the Americas Department of the Central Committee of the CPC, Manuel Pineiro, popularly known as the "Red Beard" (Barba Roja), a Sierra Maestra veteran and confidant of President Fidel Castro, arrived in Guyana in a private Cuban aircraft to support Prime Minister Burnham's initiative.

The official talks between the two parties were held at the Belfield Residence of Prime Minister Burnham. The Prime Minister led the PNC team while Dr. Cheddi Jagan headed the PPP side. The two scribes were Mr. Robert Corbin from the People's National Congress and Mr. Feroze Mohamed from the People's Progressive Party. According to Mr. Corbin, the parties were close to reaching an agreement when Mrs. Janet Jagan, a member of the PPP delegation, using the issue of National Service as the pretext to disengage from the dialogue, walked out of a crucial meeting thereby irretrievably rupturing the talks.[45] It was not until eight years later that Mr. Burnham made another serious effort, using another approach, to engage the PPP in a structured dialogue aimed at power sharing.

The 1976 initiative was very difficult for Prime Minister Burnham at the personal and political levels. For one thing, in the 1975-76 period, the PPP trade union arm, the Guyana Agricultural and General Workers Union (GAWU), called a total of 329 strikes in the sugar industry with over half million man-days lost. At the same time, there was widespread arson on the sugar estates. As Henry Jeffrey and Colin Baber have noted, "in its bid to undermine the PNC the PPP has used this union (GAWU) with devastating effect."[46] Mr. Burnham subscribed to that view to the day that he died. And the fact that the PPP was engaged in severely damaging the economy and, consequently, heightening ethnic conflict at a time when the PNC Government was under strong pressure from the West led the Prime Minister to the belief that the PPP was objectively aiding imperialism and the forces which they purported to struggle against.

Relations between the PNC and PPP leaders were, generally, cordial regardless of what was the popular perception. They met privately when the circumstances demanded it, with Mr. Burnham sharing security information with Dr. Jagan from time to time. Prime Minister Burnham quickly moved to have Dr. Jagan's personal security officers trained and armed by the Guyana Police Force when it became known that there was an external plot to harm Dr. Jagan. He kept Dr. Jagan abreast of the efforts, which the Government of Guyana was pursuing to support the Popular Movement for the Liberation of Angola (MPLA), including the re-fuelling of Cuban aircrafts in Guyana on their way to Angola. Indeed, from time to time, they discussed matters of national interest, including efforts that were being made to destabilize the Government, the bombing of the Cuban aircraft in which several Guyanese students died, and Guyana's strategy in dealing with its borders' controversies.

Historically, relations between Mr. Burnham and Mrs. Jagan have never been genuinely amicable, however. Both were wary, if not suspicious, of each other – for different reasons. In the early days of nationalist fervor, they coexisted in the interest of party and national unity. But to the PNC Leader, she was a "foreigner" who, despite her repetition of the 'ideologically correct' slogans at the time, could not harmonize with Guyanese ethos, history, and the future construction of an authentic Guyanese nation.[47] He believed that she could not be sensitive to, or genuinely appreciative of, among other things, the Guyanese religious and cultural traditions such as the Diwali and Eid festivals and the traditional African religious practices and ceremonies. Indeed, he held the view that Guyana's national motto, "One People, One Nation, One Destiny," was of no intrinsic value to Mrs. Jagan. "Her's was a different agenda," as he solemnly and tersely put it in a discussion with his senior advisers.[48]

Mr. Burnham was deeply concerned with the substantial influence, power and authority which Mrs. Jagan wielded within the PPP and, more so, over Dr. Jagan. He once remarked that important decisions reached between himself as Chairman of the PPP and Dr. Jagan as Party Leader were, on several occasions, frustrated as a result of Mrs. Jagan's subsequent intervention and he was left many a time wondering who was really the Party Leader. He mentioned that were it not for his diplomacy, level-headedness and the need for unity of the Party leadership when it was under more overt attacks from British colonialism, there would have ensued open confrontations with Mrs. Jagan as Party General Secretary for the several years that he spent in the PPP. He explained that the Party's Treasurer had little control over Party funds, which were under the direct jurisdiction of Mrs. Jagan. During his tenure as PPP Chairman, in spite of his best efforts, there was no accountability of Party's funds or examination of the Party's finances.[49]

When Mr. Burnham became Prime Minister and later President he devoted much attention to security and intelligence matters. He had extraordinary human intelligence assets at all levels of the PPP and its various arms and agencies.

He was, therefore, able to carefully monitor the activities of the PPP leadership internally and externally and to arrive at his considered judgment of those who "lived for subversion and who labored for socialism," to use his exact phrase.

Mr. Burnham was of the firmest conviction that Mrs. Jagan was deeply involved in fuelling the political and ethnic strife in the 1960's. He linked the formation of a PPP clandestine army, the Guyana Liberation Army, comprising Party activists trained in guerilla warfare, the illegal importation of weapons and explosives, the wide-spread arson on the sugar estates, the demise of the Abraham family, the explosion on the vessel Sun Chapman, and the assassination of former PPP Cuban-trained cadre, Mr. Akbar Ally, among other things, to Mrs. Jagan. Indeed, his assessment of her role in national development and in enhancing the well-being of the Guyanese people was unflattering. Above all, he was strongly convinced that she had little or no interest in power sharing and in collaborating with the Burnham Administration in its quest for national development, national unity and socialism.

But the fact that President Burnham made another attempt in 1984-85 to engage the PPP in political dialogue and power sharing tells a story, in my view, of magnanimity, pragmatism and personal concern for the national weal. And the fact that the PPP agreed once again to participate in formal political dialogue with the objective of sharing power with the PNC speaks volumes about the myth of "the dictatorial Burnham regime."

This narrative gives an unassailable insider's view of the 1984-85 unity talks. The story has to be told.

This then is that story.

President Burnham sharing a lighter moment with the late President of Mozambique, Samora Machel.

|1|

THE OBJECTIVE AND SUBJECTIVE CONDITIONS OF POLITICAL DIALOGUE

The question of political dialogue and power sharing has constituted a recurrent theme in the political history of Guyana. Apart from the 1960's and the 1970's, they have been projected in the public sphere more repeatedly and more profoundly in the aftermath of the political upheavals and the ethnic tensions of the 1997 and 2001 National and Regional Elections, and have today become a focal point of debate.

This is not the first time that that crucial issue has come to the fore. In 1961, the year the then colony of British Guiana was accorded the status of self-government, Mr. Eusi Kwayana, later to become an eminent political activist of the Working People's Alliance and one of the more prominent of Guyana's Elder Statesmen, advanced a Joint Premiership Proposal for consideration between the ruling People's Progressive Party (PPP) and the opposition People's National Congress (PNC).[50] This is believed to be the first attempt aimed at sharing political power, and concomitantly, diffusing ethnic tensions, reducing the potential for conflict, and inspiring national confidence. It met with short shrift from both sides.

In December 1962, Dr. Jagan wrote to Mr. Burnham proposing a coalition government. The exchange of correspondence between the two political leaders on this matter extended over several months. However, no agreement was reached and this effort ended in failure.

In 1963, amidst the industrial and political unrest at that time, the matter of power sharing between the two parties again entered the national domain. Mr. Duncan Sandys, the British Colonial Secretary, sought to bring the three major political parties, the People's Progressive Party, the People's National Congress and the United Force, together through the formation of a national government. This exercise met a premature ending also.

In June 1964, in the wake of the tumultuous and turbulent events occasioned by a prolonged strike in the sugar industry, called by the ruling PPP to protest the changing of the electoral system from 'first-past-the post' to Proportional Representation, the leader of the PPP, Dr. Cheddi Jagan, who was then Premier of British Guiana, proposed a power-sharing formula whereby the then Opposition PNC, headed by Mr. LFS Burnham, would be a partner in a coalition government holding a number of ministerial portfolios.[51] This effort also came to naught.

In 1976, with the political environment radically re-constituted and the People's National Congress already occupying the seat of Government for twelve years, Prime Minister LFS Burnham initiated an attempt to involve the People's Progressive Party in a type of 'popular front' dispensation. By this time, Mr. Burnham's socialist orientation was becoming more and more manifest, harmonizing, as it were, with Dr. Jagan's ideological position. Four years earlier, he had spearheaded the move by four Member-States of the Caribbean Community to grant formal diplomatic recognition to Cuba. Then in the following year, he warmly welcomed President Fidel Castro to a State Visit to Guyana; and, among other things, he conducted the business of the People's National Congress in such a way that it was being recognized as a fraternal party by socialist and communist parties worldwide as it sought to assume a vanguard role in Guyana's development. This initiative to engage the PPP in dialogue was externally inspired in part and had the blessings of the world socialist community, particularly the USSR, Cuba and the Latin American socialist and communist parties. It, too, did not come to fruition.

Dr. Jagan, by that time, however, had become enamored of the concept of a 'national front government' and in August 1977, the year of the infamous 135-day GAWU strike in the sugar industry, the People's Progressive Party, publicly proposed the formation of National Patriotic Front and National Patriotic Front Government, which would be based on "a democratic, anti-imperialist and socialist-oriented programme."[52] Socialist orientation, according to Dr. Jagan, meant the "uncompromising struggle against imperialist exploitation; bringing the anti-imperialist and antisemi-feudal democratic revolution to completion; doing away with the monopolies and the domination of foreign capital…and alliance with the socialist community."[53]

The PNC believed that this call was mere public posturing, given the fact that in the previous year the PPP leadership frustrated the political dialogue aimed at effectuating a working relationship between the two parties. Mr. Burnham viewed it as another lame stunt by Dr. Jagan to placate his "Soviet masters" and to reassure them of his communist credentials. This attempt did not materialize also.

In 1979, the outstanding Guyanese historian, intellectual, and political co-leader of the Working People's Alliance, Dr. Walter Rodney, articulated the concept of a Government of National Unity and Reconstruction, with the exclusion of the People's National Congress. This scenario, too, did not come to actualization.

Toward the latter half of 1983, President LFS Burnham undertook a more serious and comprehensive enterprise in this regard. Proceeding from his considered judgment of the prevailing objective and subjective conditions, inclusive of hemispheric realities, he instructed Mr. Elvin McDavid, Chief Political Adviser to the President, to pursue secret initiatives with the PPP leadership aimed at beginning urgent political dialogue – the ultimate purpose of which would be the sharing of governmental power with the People's Progressive Party.

At that time, I was President Burnham's Deputy Chief Political Adviser and, simultaneously, National Secretary of the Guyana Committee for Solidarity and Peace (GCSP), one of two local Peace Movements affiliated to the World Peace Council (WPC), whose President was the redoubtable Romesh Chandra from India. The other was the Guyana Peace Council (GPC) whose President and General Secretary were Dr. Jagan and Mr. Harry Ramdass, respectively. Not by accident, both Mr. McDavid and Dr. Jagan shared membership of the Presidium of the WPC concurrently. The diplomatic dexterity of Mr. Chandra had penetrated the complexities of Guyana's labyrinthine politics.

The political, economic and other circumstances, then, were vastly different from present day conditions. The prevailing international milieu was characterized by fierce superpower rivalry between the USSR and the USA. This rivalry actualized itself in the exercise of continuous ideological warfare, political, economic, and cultural competition, military confrontations executed on surrogate territory, and the perennial threat of a nuclear holocaust hanging over

Objective and subjective conditions of political dialogue

the heads of the universe's billions like the proverbial Sword of Damocles.

In Guyana, both President Burnham and PPP General Secretary, Dr. Cheddi Jagan, who was then Minority Leader in the Parliament of Guyana, had espoused the philosophy of Marxism and had set their sights on the construction of a socialist society in the backyard of the United States, as Guyana and, indeed, the Caribbean was referred to in those days.

By the time the idea of dialogue with the PPP leadership had been conceptualized and had transformed itself into a preponderating political concern in the mind of President Burnham, his United States counterpart, President Ronald Regan, was comfortably settled in the White House and had launched a vigorous anti-communist crusade, regionally and internationally. His foreign policy pursuits threatened to jettison the principles of peaceful co-existence and détente worked out by the USA and the USSR. He appeared to have taken little or no notice of the Declaration of Basic Principles of Relations,[54] which was jointly issued by President Richard Nixon and General Secretary of the Communist Party of the Soviet Union, Leonid Brezhnev in 1972, and which effectively abandoned both the Monroe and Brezhnev doctrines.[55] Indeed, President Regan made no secret of his commitment "to roll back the frontiers of communism" wherever they might exist.

In the Caribbean, disregarding the hallowed tenets of international law, he ordered the 1983 invasion of Grenada, a small CARICOM Member State, by US military forces which promptly removed the Revolutionary Military Council that has assumed the reins of government, subsequent to the execution of the country's Prime Minister,

Maurice Bishop, and the ouster of the People's Revolutionary Government of Grenada from office.

The US invasion of Grenada, in particular, and the undisguised, aggressive nature of the US Presidency, in general, greatly disturbed President Burnham. Supported by political and intelligence analyses, he came to the firm conclusion that the United States would not hesitate to intervene militarily in Guyana, if the Government persisted in pursuing policies that did not synchronize with US interests.

The PNC Leader strongly believed that the 1976 bombings of the Guyana's Consulate in Trinidad and Tobago and the Cuban aircraft in which several Guyanese were killed, the strong criticisms of the Guyana Government by the US Administration in 1980, the United States influence in blocking an Inter-American Development Bank Agricultural Sector Loan in 1981, the hostility from Venezuela on Guyana's western border, the scathing commentary by the US State Department's Country Reports on Human Rights Practices, the inauguration of the Caribbean Basin Initiative in 1982 designed to isolate socialist-oriented governments in the Caribbean and Central America, the cancellation of a US$15 million loan from USAID, and the recall of the US Ambassador in 1983, among other things, cumulatively constituted the prelude to naked aggression.

The PPP interpreted the events of the time in the following manner. "The PNC is under pressure from imperialism to end its support for national liberation movements and the non-aligned movement and to discontinue it relations with the socialist world."[56]

Prior to the US invasion of Grenada, Guyana had been slowly developing solid relations with the world socialist community, specifically the Soviet Union and Cuba. Immediately after the invasion, President Burnham sought to intensify that relationship. He began to institute a number of measures that he hoped would prevent the landing of US troops on Guyana's soil. Primary among those was the deepening of ties with the world socialist community.[57]

A few weeks after the invasion of Grenada, he dispatched a high level delegation, led by Mr. Elvin McDavid, to the USSR and Eastern Europe as one of those measures. It comprised senior functionaries from the People's National Congress, the Government of Guyana and the Guyana Defence Force. The purpose of the visit was to intensify political, economic and military cooperation with several socialist governments and to consolidate relations with the communist parties in that region. I performed the duties of Secretary to the delegation.

But although President Burnham ascribed priority to matters of national sovereignty and defense of Guyana's territorial integrity, two other issues impacted on his consciousness very profoundly.

The first was the fact that the country was retrogressing on the economic front. Indeed, it began to reel under the effects of oil price increases in 1973 and 1979, the fall in the international prices for sugar and rice in 1976-1978, the recession in the industrialized countries in the early 1980s and the debt crisis, which erupted in 1982.[58] In practical terms, this meant virtually stagnant wages and salaries for public sector employees, a decline in the productive sectors of the economy, a deficiency in foreign currency, a shortage of basic food items and other consumer goods, deterioration in public services and social infrastructure, and a higher unemployment rate, among other things.

All of these, and the ever recurring political and industrial unrest in the sugar industry, festering like an incurable sore, heightened ethnic and political division and whittled away at the fragile foundations of the national economy.

Linked inextricably to the internal problematic was an exogenous factor of fundamental importance. With the combined political, economic and military might of the United States and the United Kingdom buttressing the western capitalist structure, there had begun to emerge with greater vigor a deliberate, sustained movement towards the re-assertion of the ideological paradigm which pre-supposed the superiority of a free market system over centrally planned economies. This meant that autochthonous models of economic development, particularly those efforts at experimenting with central planning, had become liabilities and had to be supplanted – even if it meant employing covert and overt measures of aggression. Western capitalism, therefore, orchestrated and operationalized a variety of stratagems directed at destabilizing the Burnham Administration, frustrating the fledgling endeavors at socialist transformation, and re-instituting a market economy.

In the context of those external pressures and internal difficulties, President Burnham had, once again, arrived at the conclusion that his Government and the People's National Congress alone could not "defend our economy…defend the gains of our revolution," as he put it, without the intrinsic involvement of the People's Progressive Party in the administration of the State, and that Party's commitment to the re-vitalization of the national economy. In other words, given the existing national milieu shaped by the historical realities of ethnic cleavages, political differentiation, cultural affinity, and occupational preferences, the People's National

Congress all by itself would find it difficult to truly build the Guyanese nation and mould its destiny. It was Mr. Burnham's hope to recapture the nationalist spirit of the 1953 era and to lead a politically and ideologically unified people in the construction of a socialist society in his lifetime.

The second fundamental issue in which President Burnham seemed to absorb himself had to do with diminishing ethnic discord, heightening cultural respect and promoting a genuine Guyanese identity. He was not oblivious to the fact that the unity of the two major ethnic groups was still a far way off. He believed, however, that while they would in time evolve ways and means of genuinely accepting each other, socialism offered a path of hastening the pace of national unity and economic development. He held the unshakeable view that socialism was about the creation and distribution of wealth and prosperity, and that once the Guyanese people as a whole had begun to really integrate themselves in the process of being gainfully employed, building the nation and prospering individually and collectively, then the problems associated with conflicts and cleavages would be the issues furthest from their minds.

President Burnham was a realist, if he was anything. He acknowledged that a nation-state that was politically and ethnically polarized would lack the capacity to withstand and surmount the machinations of the 'colossus of the north' and, consequently, determine its own path to political economic and social development. He contended that a *modus vivendi* with the PPP would greatly assist in reducing ethnic distrust and promoting national unity, extricating the country from the economic morass in which it had found itself, resisting external pressures and constructing a new Guyanese society – all of which coincided with the

PPP's point of view.[59]

It was against the backdrop of those objective realities and subjective circumstances that secret discussions with the People's Progressive Party leadership were initiated – without the approval of the General Council of the People's National Congress.

|2|

PRELUDE TO DIALOGUE

In private discussions with President Burnham and from other available evidence, it would appear that he, if anyone, had internalized the concept of political dialogue and power sharing with the People's Progressive Party and was proceeding on a step-by-step basis to achieve that grand objective. Time and again, he was at pains to explain that his differences with the leadership of the PPP were in part due to personality problems, tactical approaches to nation building, given the geo-political realities of the time, the PPP's uncritical acceptance of the Soviet model of development and its dogmatic interpretation of socialism. But deep in his bosom he wanted a unified nation, a significant part of which looked to the PPP for leadership.

After President Burnham had instructed Mr. McDavid to begin secret talks with the PPP leadership, the first movement in the direction of structured political dialogue was the establishment of small Working Group that operated out of the Political Division of the Office of the President. It was chaired by Mr. McDavid and included Messrs. Malcolm Parris, Minister of Education; Jeffrey Thomas, Minister of Home Affairs; Patrick Denny, Head of the Department of National Orientation and International Affairs, People's National Congress and myself. Dr. Richard Van West Charles, the son-in-law of President Burnham and Minister of Health, Mr. Harun Rashid, Minister of Energy, and others attended meetings of the Working Group from time to time to share their points of view.

President Burnham had carefully supervised the composition of the Working Group. The basic qualifications for membership to that inner circle had to do with an abiding loyalty to the President's goals, a broad socialist orientation, and a genuine desire to accommodate the PPP in some mutually agreed arrangement for power sharing. In other words, he wanted a team that understood the political and ideological mind of that Party, that found it easy to relate to the Party's leading and most influential members, formally and informally, and one that would stoutly defend the PNC's position, if ever and whenever it came to that.

The role of the Working Group, in general terms, was to conceptualize broad dialogue proposals which would be submitted to the PNC's political directorate for re-fashioning and further refinement, provide informed opinions and analyses to President Burnham, and to interface with various levels of the PPP leadership on behalf of the PNC when the necessity arose.

The second measure, which President Burnham decided upon, was that since time was of the essence, the Working Group should strive assiduously to establish early contact with the PPP in order to commence the process of dialogue. He indicated that such contact should start at the level of the Peace Committees, which, in his opinion, would convey to the Working Group whether or not the PPP was inclined to have any discussion at all with the PNC leadership.

Dialogue, especially serious political deliberations, can only fructify in a climate of mutual trust, understanding and confidence. Years of bitter political antagonisms between the PNC and the PPP had done nothing to create such a climate and thus that barrier had to be surmounted. The Working Group recognized that stark reality and, after substantial debate, concluded that Mr. McDavid, who was also President of the GCSP, should – after talking with Dr. Jagan privately – send a formal letter to him in his capacity as President of the GPC suggesting that the two Peace Movements should consider coordinating their activities and collaborating in areas of mutual concern.

That letter, dispatched to Dr. Jagan in April 1984, stated, among other things, that US imperialism had again become overtly hostile to governments which were seeking to pursue a socialist path of development, that counter-revolutionary forces were bent on destabilizing the Government of Guyana and eliminating the principal leaders of the PNC and the PPP, that the two Peace Movements should develop common programs and, that given all of the foregoing, the GCSP was proposing that there should be discussions with the GPC in the national interest.

The PPP General Secretary responded positively. He concurred with the thrust of Mr. McDavid's letter and declared that he was amenable to suggestions on cooperating with the GCSP. This response, naturally, created a comfortable basis for communication between both organizations allowing them to amplify on the issues contained in Mr. McDavid's letter and to explore the opportunities for personal contact and further confidence building measures.

Mr. Burnham was later fully briefed on Dr. Jagan's reply and the telephone conversations between Mr. McDavid and Dr. Jagan that followed. Mr. McDavid also advised the PNC Leader on the reactions and perceptions of the Resident Ambassadors of the Soviet Union, the German Democratic Republic and Cuba, who had been apprised of the proposed cooperation between the GCSP and GPC. He was further kept up to date with the informal discourses that had begun to take place between some members of the Working Group and members of the PPP Political Bureau, and other pertinent matters. Mr. Burnham, subsequently, instructed that a third stage be embarked upon – the level of personal contact between emissaries of the GCSP and the GPC.

The Working Group advanced the notion that, as a General Secretary of the GCSP, I should prepare myself psychologically and otherwise to initiate formal discussions with Mr. Harry Ramdass, the GPC General Secretary. Obviously, that required the approval of Mr. Burnham, who was not unaware of my personal and professional relationship, cultivated years ago, with my GPC counterpart.

Mr. Ramdass had served as Headmaster of Cotton Tree Government School, West Coast Berbice, in the late 1960's where I also taught at the same time as Assistant Master. At that time, also, he used to live at D'Edward Village, just under a mile from where I resided. Our families developed a close relationship and he and I formed an amicable and enduring camaraderie.

In the circumstances, Mr. Burnham thought that I was an excellent choice to meet with the PPP envoy. Rather swiftly, Mr. McDavid informed Dr. Jagan of the GCSP nominee and, in a matter of weeks, Mr. Ramdass and I began meeting at his home in Upper Robb Street, Bourda, Georgetown.

Those encounters, comprising an admixture of bonhomie and seriousness, were extremely significant from the point of view of the Working Group and, I believe, the PPP. They demonstrated, if only in a tentative way, that the PNC was intent on building bridges of cooperation for the purposes of securing the national well-being; they confirmed that the ruling political directorate was willing to surmount political differences in order to enhance the national weal; and they signaled in no uncertain terms that President Burnham, as the maximum leader of the Party and Government, had transcended personal sensitivities and private susceptibilities so as to create an environment that would engender national unity and dignity.

After a while, with confidence emerging more and more on both sides, the Working Group sought to widen the point of contact with the GPC thereby advancing the discussions from the personal to the organizational level. Thereafter, a GCSP Negotiating Team was constituted. It comprised Mr. Patrick Denny, Mr. Michael Scott, whose substantive post was Political Affairs Officer in the Political Division of the Office of the President, and myself. We developed a solid rapport with our colleagues on the other side. Generally, they appeared to be genuinely interested in carrying forward the preliminary dialogue to a higher level, which coincided with our fundamental aim. We encouraged that idea and sought to reinforce their confidence in that direction for we knew fully that it was not going to be easy for them to convince their comrades in the People's Progressive Party to enter into a political partnership with the People's National Congress.

In the meantime, President Burnham was being frequently apprised of the emergent scenario by Mr. McDavid and, of course, through special operatives drawn from the Police Special Branch. At the behest of the President, Mr. McDavid continued to brief the Ambassadors from the Soviet Union, the German Democratic Republic and Cuba, from time to time.

But President Burnham seemed to be in a great hurry to accomplish what he had embarked upon.

He demanded that the Group engage itself in overtime work so that it could draw up fresh proposals, which, after careful study, would be submitted to Dr. Jagan for his consideration – the broad aim being to give life-support to the process that had assumed form, and to generate interest and momentum. Premised on the conversations that had already taken place, President Burnham ratified the following program of action:

- A team, comprising Mr. McDavid, Mr. Patrick Denny and I, would engage in talks with senior members of the PPP on any matters on which they needed to ventilate their opinions. At the same time, the PNC side would advert to issues that were likely to jeopardize the climate of the discussions and to resolve them before they were transformed into imponderables.
- The GCSP and the GPC would undertake joint solidarity activities on a continuing basis, with the Government publicly identifying with them in the form of media coverage and operational support.
- The PNC's official organ, the New Nation, would cease publication of all articles that attacked the PPP and its affiliates as a matter of deliberate policy.
- The Political Division of the Office of the President would ensure that the PPP and its affiliated organizations, among them the Progressive Youth Organization (PYO), the Women's Political Organization (WPO), the Guyana Agricultural and General Worker's Union (GAWU), and the New Guyana Company Limited, printers and publishers of the Mirror, were facilitated in their operations by the State.

Consequent on the above directions, Mr. McDavid and Mr. Clement Rohee, the PPP's Secretary for International Affairs, discussed on May 30, 1984, the urgency for formal dialogue between the PNC and the PPP at leadership level. Further to this encounter, Mr. McDavid held extensive conversations with Dr. Cheddi Jagan during the period September 25-30, 1984, on the occasion of the Guyana Trades Union Congress Annual Conference at the Critchlow Labour College.

On November 30, 1984, Mr. Denny kept an important rendezvous with Mr. Rohee to exchange views on critical areas of concern to the PPP. Mr. Rohee raised two significant issues. He seemed to be pushing for the discourses between the GCSP and the GPC to include "broader political matters" to which Mr. Denny pointed out that "the arrangements which were worked out between Comrades Ramdass and Majeed provided for the inclusion of any topic and for the appropriate additions to the two teams."[60] Mr. Rohee also wondered whether discussions could not take place between the two Peace Movements and the two Parties simultaneously. Mr. Denny found no difficulty with that position adding that, at the Peace Committee level, they could focus on "working out ways of cooperation in the anti-imperialist struggle, and at the political level on elements of national development..."[61]

In a comment as to the level at which the political deliberations should take place, Mr. Rohee indicated that, having read the transcripts of the unity talks between the leadership of the two Parties in 1976, he felt that the leaders should not be involved in the initial stages but should come into the picture if serious and fundamental difficulties arose between the negotiating teams. Mr. Denny submitted that his side's view was that they should be seen as a kind of Court of Appeal, which would be resorted to, if and when intractable positions were adopted on both sides. He reiterated that whatever level was convenient for the PPP "we stand ready to engage in meaningful discussions."[62]

Meanwhile, leading PNC and PPP officials had re-commenced speaking with each other whenever they met at various social gatherings, particularly at Receptions hosted by the Embassies of the USSR, Cuba and the GDR. The political acrimony had begun to recede in a small way.

By this time, President Burnham had formally briefed members of the Central Executive Committee of the People's National Congress on the rapport that had been effectuated with the People's Progressive Party. In pursuing that step, the PNC Leader sought to commit the wider leadership of the Party intrinsically to the new process that was unfolding and to harness their energies in that direction. He needed to re-shape their convictions early on the exclusivity of state power and to re-orient them towards a policy of inclusion. Thereafter, as Commander-in-Chief, he also advised the high command of the Disciplined Services[63] of the political initiative that he had begun to pursue in relation to the PPP.

Both the Central Executive Committee and the leadership of the Disciplined Services unanimously endorsed the initiative.

The Working Group, in the meantime, had amplified on the four-point action program, which was being implemented gradually. It recommended to the President and the Central Executive Committee the following tactical approaches for their consideration:

- The GCSP and the GPC should intensify their activities throughout the country on a joint platform in order to indicate to their constituencies that a process of rapprochement between the Government and the Opposition was underway.
- The PNC and the PPP should begin to take practical steps to effect a cessation of overt political hostilities relative to each other so that an environment favorable to dialogue could be created. Translated into the realm of practice, this meant ending political strikes and arson in the sugar industry, desisting from physical attacks on members of both Party, and refraining from undue criticisms of each other in the media, among other things.
- The PNC and the PPP should give serious thought to the formulation, implementation and monitoring of a National Program for Economic, Social and Cultural Development to be ratified in Parliament with the aim of reinforcing the notion of inclusive governance.
- The PNC and the PPP should seek to devise innovative methods that would lead to the joint management of the ten Regional Democratic Councils in order to demonstrate devolution of political power.
- The PNC and the PPP should work out various ways and means of cooperation at the level of Central Government in order to establish a mood of reconciliation and to replace the prevailing environment of conflict.

In early January 1985, the People's National Congress convened its first General Council meeting for that year.

The General Council, under the Constitution of the Party, is the second highest forum of the People's National Congress – the Biennial Congress being the highest. It comprises representatives from the Party's arms, District and Regional Committees, other bodies of the Party, and PNC Members of Parliament. Senior Government officials, regardless of party affiliation, and high-ranking members of the Disciplined Services are invited to attend as Special Invitees also, since that forum seeks to formulate general policies for the consideration of Government.

That meeting was a milestone event in the life of the PNC. Convened primarily for discussing the issue of political dialogue and power sharing with the PPP, the most significant item on the agenda was the Presentation delivered by the indefatigable Deputy Leader and Chairman of the Central Executive Committee of the Party, Dr. Ptolemy Alexander Reid.[64]

In his address, Dr. Reid analyzed the international political and economic situation, particularly the role of imperialism in relation to developing nations. He examined the domestic milieu and assessed what the Party and Government had achieved under extremely difficult circumstances. He traced the evolution of the Guyanese nation, adverting to the historical bonds that linked the different ethnic groups, the cultural diversity that enriched the national mosaic, and the common sacrifices, which, among other things, have forged a strong, resilient people. Long before Prof. Ali Mazrui of Tanzania had said it, Dr. Reid exhorted the audience to have "short memories of hate" since it was not a palatable ingredient for national development. Finally, in calling for greater unity among Guyanese, he declared that "the People's National Congress should now purse a policy of constructive dialogue with the People's Progressive Party on a structured party-to-party basis so that the process of socialist construction could be intensified."[65] He concluded

Prelude to dialogue

that "we are now trying to carry out a program for genuine development in the face of mighty enemies and so new relationships have to be established…this is now very important."[66]

Dr. Reid's remarks received a thundering, prolonged ovation. It was as though he had articulated the aspirations and hopes of the General Council membership, saying the very words that the members had themselves wanted to say. One after the other, Regional, District and other stalwarts of the Party's leadership took to the floor and eloquently supported the new policy that had been enunciated. In the end, it secured the unanimous endorsement of the General Council.

Another rung of the Party's leadership had sanctioned President Burnham's initiative thereby widening approval for the embryonic project. This injected a dynamic of its own into the overall process and Party groups, members and supporters from far and wide began commending the President on his innovative statecraft, as they began looking at the PPP from a new perspective. It was in this context that the Working Group was instructed to craft a letter, which was to be submitted to the Party's Central Executive Committee, for vetting and onward transmission to the People's Progressive Party.

On January 25, 1985, Dr. Reid, in his capacity as Deputy Leader and Chairman of the Central Executive Committee, wrote the Central Committee of the People's Progressive Party formally proposing dialogue at the leadership level between the Parties. The letter pointed to the aggressive nature of imperialism at the international level; it alluded to the political situation in Central America and the Caribbean, and it outlined the external pressures that were being imposed on the Guyana Government for laying the foundations of socialism. It also noted the sequence of occurrences that had engaged the two parties in the search for accommodation and conciliation. Remarking upon the expectations of the Guyanese working class and working people for a better tomorrow and, ultimately, a just society, the letter ended by stating that "the People's National Congress extends the hand of friendship and unity to the People's Progressive Party. History will judge this offer and your Party's response to it."[67]

Mr. Denny and I delivered that letter by hand to Freedom House, headquarters of the PPP.

A little after two weeks, on February 11, 1985, Dr. Jagan replied to Dr. Reid, on behalf of the PPP Central Committee. The PPP leadership wanted to consult with the Party's membership before giving an answer to the PNC, Dr. Jagan declared. In addition, he asked that the PPP be provided with "specific suggestions" for cooperation.

In this instance, the PPP General Secretary was pursuing the very opposite course of that undertaken by the PNC Leader. Whereas President Burnham first sought to convince his Party's leadership of the imperatives for dialogue with the PPP, Dr. Jagan thought it best to confer with Party members, to invoke the principles of democratic centralism – not so much "to secure the approval of the PPP membership, but to give the semblance of consultation and debate and to play for time."[68]

In the meantime, a not insignificant complication had in reality arisen within the PPP. The Police Special Branch Intelligence Reports to President Burnham indicated that for some time there had apparently emerged in the Party two factions: the "pro-unity" group and the "anti-unity" group.

Prelude to dialogue

The former was symbolized by Dr. Jagan and comprised Mr. Feroze Mohamed, Mr. Clement Rohee, Mr. Moses Nagamootoo, and Mr. Clinton Collymore, in the main. The latter included Mrs. Jagan, Mr. Narbada Persaud, Mr. Rohit Persaud, Mr. Navin Chandarpal, Mr. Fazal Ally, Mr. Neil Kumar and a few others in the lower ranks of the Party.

The anti-unity faction's position was that President Burnham was engaging the PPP in a cosmetic exercise and it appeared to nurture a pathological fear that Dr. Jagan would be outmaneuvered by the PNC Leader if he entered into any dialogue with Mr. Burnham. According to the reports, Mrs. Jagan believed that President Burnham had succeeded in duping President Castro and the Communist Party of Cuba but he would never hoodwink her with his Marxist sophistry. She made it clear that she was neither enamored of Cuba's relations with the PNC nor with Mr. Burnham's new socialist credentials. The reports consistently stated that she continued to harp on the idea of punishing the PNC and to harbor notions of removing the PNC Government by more "revolutionary" means.

The pro-unity group's attitude, particularly that of Dr. Jagan, was that the PPP should have an open mind on the matter of political dialogue and power sharing with the PNC. The other members especially Mr. Feroze Mohamed privately concurred with Dr. Jagan's 1975 position that the PNC had put socialism on the agenda in Guyana but they were afraid to publicly take a strong stand against Mrs. Jagan since she controlled the appointments and promotions in the Party, attendance at overseas conferences, access to Party scholarships and the finances of the Party.

With the full knowledge of the intra-party conflict, President Burnham continued his effort in the direction of political dialogue.

In his response to Dr. Jagan's communication, Dr. Reid, on March 14, 1985, mentioned that the PNC's proposal envisaged the establishment of inter-party structures that "would enable either party to raise, discuss and process matters for cooperation." He reiterated the PNC's position to proceed with the establishment of a Preparatory Committee that could commence discussions immediately on the "modalities, procedural matters, and other issues relevant to the proposed formal dialogue at leadership level as soon as your party wishes." [69]

Between March and May of that year, the PPP convened three one-day County Conferences to discuss the PNC's call for political dialogue. According to the reports from the Police Special Branch, which were submitted to President Burnham, the Party's senior spokesmen, particularly Mr. Feroze Mohamed, were able to marshal very strong arguments in favor of accepting the PNC's invitation, and their point of view prevailed. All three Country Conferences voted unanimously for political dialogue and power sharing.

On May 20, 1985, Dr. Jagan, acting upon Dr. Reid's second letter, indicated, among other things, that "having completed the necessary discussions and consultations, the Executive Committee of the People's Progressive Party wish to inform you that we are prepared to enter into discussions with you on a formal basis." His letter also suggested that "a Committee made up of two members from each of our Parties meet, at a mutually agreed on time and place, to work out the technical aspects related to these talks." [70]

Prelude to dialogue

In a related development, the Office of the President afterwards issued a Press Statement on May 24, 1985, explaining that the PPP had responded to the PNC's call for constructive dialogue on a structured Party-to-Party basis at leadership level.[71]

On May 31, 1985, Dr. Reid advised the PPP General Secretary by way of another correspondence that "although my Party would have been inclined to suggest that each side should be represented by three members on the Preparatory Committee, we accept your suggestion that the number of members should be two on each side." He identified Mr. Ranji Chandisingh, PNC General Secretary and Vice-President, and Mr. Elvin McDavid, Member of the PNC Central Executive Committee, as the PNC representatives who would constitute that Party's team. He also named me as the contact person with whom the PPP could discuss the "time and place of meetings of the Preparatory Committee."[72]

The PPP selected Mr. Feroze Mohamed, Member of Parliament and Member of the Executive Committee, and Mr. Clement Rohee, Secretary for International Affairs, as its plenipotentiaries to the Preparatory Committee.

It was agreed by both sides that I should be the official scribe at the meetings.

The stage was now set for formal dialogue – after nearly two years of delicate and painstaking labors.

I contacted Freedom House, subsequently, and it was mutually decided that the first meeting of the Preparatory Committee would be held on July 19, 1985, at 11:00 a.m. in the Committee Room of the National Assembly, Georgetown.

Forbes Burnham

THE START OF THE DIALOGUE PROCESS

The first meeting of the Preparatory Committee was very cordial. The political adversaries were no strangers to each other. Mr. Chandisingh was the Deputy Leader of the People's Progressive Party prior to his resignation from the PPP in 1976. I, myself, was one time Chairman of the Progressive Youth Organization, youth arm of the PPP, succeeding the late Mr. Vincent Teekah. Mr. McDavid, who initiated the secret talks, had developed a close camaraderie with Mr. Mohamed and Mr. Rohee. And so the two sides set about their emergent enterprise with a combination of cordiality and optimism, perhaps cognizant of the fact that that they were pioneers in sowing the seeds of a potentially new political culture.

Calling the historic meeting to order, and speaking on behalf of the People's National Congress, Mr. Chandisingh observed that the Burnham Initiative sought to engage in constructive political dialogue and to effectuate power sharing with the People's Progressive Party. It was endorsed by the Party's leadership and its broader membership, and it must be construed as a fundamental and genuine effort to involve the People's Progressive Party in the process of national development and socialist construction. He observed that the process to engage the PPP in a structured dialogue was quietly started more than a year ago with no certainty that is would come to a positive conclusion. However, he added, through President Burnham's persistence, optimism and statesmanship, "we are meeting you in friendship today, without any pre-conditions, in this hallowed precinct, the National Assembly, thereby signifying that we are treating this matter with all the seriousness and respect it deserves."[73]

He remarked that the path on which the two Parties had embarked would not be without difficulties but he was confident that the vital interests and the similarity of goals, which had brought them together, would take precedence over political prejudice and personal feelings. He made a fervent plea for the successful outcome of the Preparatory Committee's deliberations, which, he hoped, would lead to dialogue at a higher stage.

Mr. Clement Rohee, in replying to Mr. Chandisingh's remarks, lauded the Burnham Initiative and observed that it augured well for unifying the Guyanese working class and working people. He declared that the PPP had always striven for national unity and would continue to do so through whatever legitimate avenues were at its disposal. He mentioned that Dr. Jagan and the PPP were not interested in power for the sake of power, but for strengthening the working class and the working people of the country in order to build a society based on the principles of scientific socialism. The PPP International Affairs Secretary submitted that dialogue between political opponents was never an easy task but, in the prevailing circumstances, the PPP would adopt an optimistic and a realistic position.[74]

From the discussions and debate that ensued at the meeting, it would appear that the PPP had been considering rather profoundly the notion of political dialogue and power sharing with the PNC. Indeed, it would seem that its leadership had devoted substantial time and toil to the proposed project, for their representatives' thoughts were clear and constructive. Without rancor or acrimony, the meeting adopted the following decisions:

Firstly, it was agreed that the Preparatory Committee would settle the modalities and procedures relating to the work of other Committees, which, of necessity, would have to be established; concur on the size and structure of those Committees; and finally dissolve itself having completed those assignments.

Secondly, it was agreed that the Preparatory Committee would meet in the Committee Room of the National Assembly until its work was finished, and that other Committees, when constituted, could utilize BIDCO House, State House, the Ogle Government House or Parliament Building, which the Government would make available upon request.

Thirdly, it was agreed that the two sides would submit in writing their perceptions of the type of organizational structure that should be employed for the conduct of the dialogue between the People's National Congress and the People's Progressive Party. This conclusion was reached in view of the divergence of opinions, which surfaced and could not be reconciled at the meeting. Both sides advanced certain tentative proposals.

Mr. Elvin McDavid, one of the PNC representatives, suggested a four-tired configuration as follows:

- An Inter-Party Preparatory Team, which would determine the agenda items that would be the subject of debate at the meetings of the Principal Team conducting the discussions;

- An Inter-Party Commission which would comprise the substantive body that would articulate definitive positions and reach binding conclusions;
- An Inter-Party Liaison Group that would aim at resolving thorny or sensitive issues;
- An Inter-Party Summit that would be the final arbiters in the dialogue.

Mr. Feroze Mohamed of the People's Progressive Party argued for a three-pronged arrangement as follows:

- An Inter-Party Committee;
- Inter-Party Sub-Committees that would examine specific issues as designated by the Inter-Party Preparatory Committee;
- The Inter-Party Group that would include the two Party Leaders, and would be the substantive body that would conduct the talks.

Fourthly, the meeting agreed, *in toto*, that it was absolutely essential for the dialogue to be nurtured in a climate of congeniality. After a very candid debate, it was resolved that the PNC side would provide the PPP with "written proposals which could be used as a basis for discussion."

Fifthly, the participants agreed that, in the initial stages, the discussions that constituted the dialogue process, including the deliberations of the Preparatory Committee, should be of a confidential nature. Prior to that, Mr. Rohee had vigorously contended that his personal thinking on the matter was that they ought to be brought into the public arena. Mr. Chandisingh posited that the People's National Congress would have no objection to acquainting the public with the progress of the talks from time to time. He, however, asserted that the two Parties should jointly release any

The start of the dialogue process

information that would be disseminated to the public simultaneously. This procedure, he argued, would serve to eliminate contradictions and avoid confusion.

Sixthly, the participants agreed that Notes of Meetings would be mutually agreed upon and initialed by both sides.

Finally, the participants agreed that a Press Release should be issued in order to signal to the public that a process of rapprochement between the People's National Congress and the People's Progressive Party had officially begun.

The first official encounter between the two Parties — the product of long moments of maneuvers — after nine years, ended on a note of cautious optimism.

But much work lay ahead. The minutes of the meeting had to be prepared and approved by both sides, the Press Release had to be crafted and agreed upon by both sides, proposals for the organizational framework within which the dialogue would be conducted had to be drafted and exchanged, and submissions relating to the creation of the type of environment that would be expected to prevail during the course of the dialogue had to be formulated and exchanged also.

In terms of the Press Release, Mr. Feroze Mohamed and I quickly settled for a two-paragraph statement. The full text, which was published in the Sunday Chronicle of July 21, 1985, ran as follows:

"Following upon the exchange of letters between the PNC and the PPP with respect to talks between the two parties, the Preparatory Committee, which was mutually agreed to, met for the first time on Friday 19th July. This Committee's task is primarily to work out the procedures, the agenda and the general

framework in which the two-party talks are to proceed.

"At its first meeting, the Committee discussed broadly several questions related to its task. Both sides advanced views on the structure for the talks and offered suggestions for their positive development. In the course of the discussions, there were several points of coincidence while others are to be further considered and discussed."

In the meantime, the PNC Central Executive Committee had established a high level monitoring mechanism to directly oversee all aspects of the "unity talks," as they came to be called. It comprised the Party Leader (Mr. L.F.S. Burnham), the Deputy Leader (Dr. Ptolemy Reid), the General Secretary (Mr. Ranji Chandisingh), the Prime Minister (Mr. H.D. Hoyte), the Attorney General (Dr. Mohamed Shahabuddin), and the Chief Political Adviser to the President (Mr. Elvin McDavid). Simultaneously, the Deputy Leader was delegated to brief the Central Executive Committee on the progress of the talks from time to time.

|4|

THE POWER SHARING CONFIGURATION

At the national level, the People's National Congress was in the final stages of preparing for its Sixth Biennial Congress scheduled to be held from August 18 through August 25, 1985, at the Sophia Auditorium, Greater Georgetown. The dialogue between the PNC and the PPP was expected to be a major topic of the Party Leader's Opening Address and the deliberations of Congress. Simultaneously, the Party was organizing and mobilizing for the National and Regional Elections scheduled to be held later that year.

At the same time, President Burnham was feverishly contemplating the implementation of several measures, which he considered were crucial to the well-being of the nation, given the changing political environment. Among those were the re-organization of the People's National Congress, the Government machinery, including the Public Corporations, and the Disciplined Services; increasing the efficiency of the Public Service; the combating of corruption on a wider and deeper scale; the re-importation of wheaten flour in the country as official policy; the deepening of economic and trading relationships with the socialist countries, including Cuba; securing military support from the socialist countries to boost Guyana's defense capabilities; and above all, the introduction of novel political arrangements that would accommodate the People's Progressive Party in a power sharing configuration, which, he strongly believed, would accelerate the pace of national development.

In the last regard, he tasked the Working Group with enunciating a power sharing formula that would complement the other propositions which had been already conceptualized for the dialogue.

The Working Group drew up a secret document titled, *"Some Tentative Proposals for the Formation of a United Fatherland Front of Guyana."*[75] It contained preliminary thoughts on a power sharing paradigm involving mainly the PNC and the PPP. That document outlined the imperatives for the formation of a Fatherland Front, the definition and composition of that body, its aims and objectives, the organizational structure of the Front, and the organization of the Government of the Fatherland Front.

At the time, the Working Group was neither overly concerned nor pre-occupied with the theoretical aspects of power sharing. In the circumstances, it could not afford to indulge in the luxury of academic debates. Its paramount objective was to involve the competing political actors in a practical mode of governance that would benefit the nation.

The United Fatherland Front, as the document conceived of it in those historical circumstances, would consist of the political parties represented in the National Assembly, the trade unions, religious organizations, women's and youth groups, civic associations and similar bodies. It would be organized on the basis of District Committees, Regional Committees and the Central Committee, with the last being the highest forum of the Fatherland Front.

A Central Coordinating Committee and a full time Permanent Secretariat would service the Central Committee.

The actual numbers that would constitute the various Committees would be arrived at by consensus among the political parties and other organizations.

It was clearly recognized that the General Secretary of the PPP, Dr. Cheddi Jagan, would head the Central Committee, while an appointee of the PNC would be designated Secretary-General of the Central Committee.

The Government of Guyana would be the executive arm of the Fatherland Front in keeping with the presumption that the Front would be the paramount political entity in the country.

In any national elections, it was envisaged that the Fatherland Front would field a joint list of candidates that would contest such elections.

The Government would be organized as follows:

1. **The National Assembly**, which would be the highest governmental forum in the land;

2. **The Supreme Congress of the People**, which would be an advisory body to the National Assembly;

3. **The Council of State**, which would be the most important component of Government, and which would be composed of the President of the Republic, Vice-Presidents, and other designated representatives of the State;

4. **The Council of Ministers**, which would implement the decisions of the Council of State and the National Assembly, and which would be chaired by the Head of State or his nominee.

The foregoing ideas were, indeed, very broad, very tentative formulations. It was anticipated that they would form the basis of rather substantial discussions by the People's National Congress at all levels before it became an official ument that would be transmitted to the People's Progressive Party leadership for their examination and analyses.

The Working Group submitted this document to President Burnham and to members of the Party's Central Executive Committee for their comments and impressions. It was hoped that with their studied input and collective wisdom, the First Draft would be used as a theoretical basis for seriously analyzing the question of power sharing in fundamental terms with the People's Progressive Party.

By July 22, 1985, the Notes of the first Preparatory Committee Meeting were ready for scrutiny by the PPP plenipotentiaries. At the same time, it was foreseen that a more detailed joint Press Statement would be published simultaneously in the **New Nation**, official organ of the PNC and the **Sunday Mirror**, the PPP weekly, on July 28, 1985. However, the actual text of the Press Statement became the subject of mild controversy and its settlement was turned into a stretched out affair. Neither Party had the least idea of the impending catastrophe that was about to descend on the nation and which would turn the ideological wheel full circle from cooperative socialism to capitalism. Nor was it anticipated that the dialogue process would be a transitory phenomenon etched perhaps only in the minds of the primary actors of that political drama.

Early Monday, August 5, 1985, President Burnham telephoned me on my hot line to meet him at his Belfield Residence. By the time I arrived there, he had traveled to the Vlissingence Road Residence where, apparently, he had forgotten that he had summoned me. At the Residence he appeared not to be fully organized - which was absolutely uncharacteristic of him. He informed me that he wanted to meet Mr. McDavid and me that night in his office at the Presidential Secretariat.

Again, at the meeting that evening, something seemed amiss. I put it down then to the impending surgical procedure that President Burnham was to undergo early the next day. Mr. McDavid and I tried to assuage his apparent anxiety by the usual friendly banter we would have with him. However, perhaps unbeknownst to the President, he was having his final meeting with us. We talked about the PPP Congress which was being held at that time and we discussed the dialogue process with the PPP. In turn, he posed a number of searching, rhetorical questions on various aspects of the PNC's tactics and proposed that the Working Group should ventilate its views on them and report to him during the course of the Party's Congress. Before the meeting ended, he advised us to be patient, and instructed us to spare no effort in ensuring that the unity talks were successful, since the very future of Guyana depended on their positive outcome.

The following morning on that fateful day, August 6, 1985, President Burnham was admitted to the Public Hospital Georgetown for what the doctors described as a minor surgical procedure for his throat. By mid-morning, Mr. Patrick Denny and I were engaged in discussions in my office at the Presidential Secretariat with delegates from Czechoslovakia who were in Guyana to participate in the Twenty Second Congress of the People's Progressive Party. One of the subjects in which they exhibited the most interest was the dialogue between the PNC and the PPP. Unhappily, I was compelled to terminate the meeting rather suddenly. I received word that President Burnham had died unexpectedly in the course of the surgery. Immediately, Mr.

Denny, Dr. Burton Gajadhar, Assistant Economic Adviser to the President, and I proceeded to the Hospital.

The news of the sudden death of President Burnham sent shock waves throughout the country and the farther afield. The country was plunged into a state of national mourning as the People's National Congress and the Government suffered a terrible trauma, albeit temporarily. Recovering almost instantaneously, however, the two institutions acted promptly. With Dr. Mohamed Shahabudeen, Vice-President and Attorney General, handling the legalities of the transition of the Presidency, and Ms. Celina Harewood, Senior Confidential Secretary to the President, ably supporting his efforts, Mr. Hugh Desmond Hoyte, S.C., Prime Minister and First Vice-President, was sworn in as President of the Republic and subsequently, that afternoon was elected unanimously as Leader of the People's National Congress by the Central Executive Committee of the Party.

In the immediate aftermath of President Burnham's sudden demise, Dr. Jagan raised the matter of the unity talks shortly before the former President's interment when he visited Mr. McDavid's residence to express his personal and his Party's condolences. As their discourse progressed into the night, the PPP General Secretary wondered about the prospects of the dialogue. He remarked that while he had an historical relationship with President Burnham, he merely knew the incumbent Head of State through parliamentary association. Dr. Jagan declared that he wanted to be frank and stated that while he very much wanted the dialogue to proceed with the PNC he had serious reservations about its continuity under Mr. Hoyte.

Exuding extreme optimism, Mr. McDavid assured the PPP General Secretary that the new PNC Leader was privy to all of the discussions on the subject, that the principles underlying the dialogue had been transformed into an institutionalized objective, and that the whole notion of the unity talks was more consequential than any single individual. He averred that as soon as the period of mourning was over, and the Party's Congress activities concluded, he would seek to persuade the Deputy Leader, Dr. Ptolemy Reid, and the General Secretary, Mr. Ranji Chandisingh, to employ their combined authority in securing an audience with President Hoyte for the sole purpose of obtaining his directions on the subject.

The PNC's Sixth Biennial Congress proceeded as planned. In his Opening Address to the delegates and observers, President Desmond Hoyte alluded directly to the unity talks. He declared:

"Comrades, believing, as we do, in PEACE NOT CONFLICT, we have initiated a formal dialogue with the People's Progressive Party, the main minority political interest group in this country. On the 25th January, 1985, our Deputy Leader, acting on the instructions of the Central Executive Committee, sent a letter to the Leader of the PPP, inviting that Party to begin constructive talks with us on the possibilities of cooperating in mutually identified areas of national life to promote the welfare of the Guyanese people and protect the national interest.

"For us, that invitation was a genuine one. We do not seek to gain any public relations benefit from it. We do not need to do that since, of course, we are proceeding from a position of strength. Because we are faithful to the provisions of our Constitution and the ideals of our Party, we seek to build in this country a society that can resolve its differences not through conflict and

confrontation but through cooperation and consensus. Indeed, our Constitution confers the right and imposes the duty on all citizens to participate in the work of building our country.

"It was against this background that the letter was sent. Indeed, it was not the beginning of an initiative, but rather a stage in the process of continual contacts which were being made at an informal level for some time. The Central Executive Committee of the Party was of the opinion that if anything positive was to eventuate, we should eschew secretiveness and proceed in a formal, open and public way. The preliminaries to those talks have started; they have not gone any great distance; but our Party remains committed to the idea of dialogue.

"We hope that the PPP will recognize that the interests and welfare of the Guyanese masses and the safety of our people will be best served by cooperation with us. In the final analysis, the Party is seeking to give the members of the PPP an opportunity and ample scope to play a substantial and meaningful role in the national life and involve itself fully in the constructive work of developing our country. In the national interest, we will always keep the door open for them to enter honorably into the arena of nation building. If they approach the talks in the same spirit of national interest which we have, I am confident that the outcome will be a success for us all."[76]

Early September 1985, subsequent to a lengthy discourse with Mr. McDavid, PPP representative, Mr. Clement Rohee, submitted to the PNC his Party's thoughts on the composition of the Sub-Committees and the Inter-Party Commission, which the PPP team had advanced at the first meeting of the Preparatory Committee, and their draft Terms of Reference.[77] However, the PNC did not reciprocate its ideas as promised. Mr. Rohee pressed the issue further. In a note dated September 27, 1985, to Mr. McDavid the PPP Secretary for International Affairs, made it clear that "we are still awaiting your ideas on the question of what should be the climate that is expected to prevail during the course of the talks."

Unbeknownst to the PPP, the members of the Working Group had carefully ruminated on that concern and had arrived at some preliminary conclusions sometime prior to President Burnham's passing. It was their considered judgment that the situation warranted that the PNC adopt a more aggressive and radical stand, and demonstrate that it was indeed assuming a qualitative transformation at both the Party and Government levels. The Working Group felt that the PNC must no longer be falsely perceived as a refuge for deviants and recalcitrants of one shade or another. In other words, there must be solid, iron cast evidence that the 'Party of a new type' was taking shape.

In a draft document circulated to President Burnham and members of the PNC Central Executive Committee, the Group presented the following "revolutionary propositions"[78] for their examination:

1. The PNC should continue to facilitate the PPP's request for assistance and to ensure that such requests are dealt with in a more expeditious manner.

2. The PNC should seek to convince Minority Leader, Dr. Cheddi Jagan, to establish his constitutional office and execute his duties and obligations in accordance with the provisions of the Constitution, and should impress upon him the necessity for himself and the PPP to participate in national events.

3. The PNC should take the initiative to expand the dialogue process through meetings between the women and

youth arms of both Parties and the Friendship Societies affiliated to both Parties.

4. The PNC should obtain a commitment from the PPP to refrain from taking undue political and industrial action in the sugar industry and instead seek to resolve problems affecting sugar workers at the appropriate political level.

5. The PNC should secure a firm undertaking from the PPP to accept directorships on, and to participate actively in, the work of the Boards of Public Corporation and other Government-appointed Commissions and Agencies.

6. The PNC should solicit from the PPP the unconditional agreement that allows its stalwarts, who have faithfully served the country in various governmental and other positions, to accept National Awards.[79]

7. The PNC should persuade the PPP to publicly express its recognition of the Guyana National Service and the Guyana People's Militia and prevail upon its members and supporters to join all branches of the Disciplined Services, including the Guyana Defense Force, the Guyana Police Force and the Guyana Fire Service.

8. The PNC should ensure that the PPP have meaningful access to the national media in order to canvas its points of view and preach its ideology.

9. The PNC should establish a high-profiled agency, an Inspectorate, possibly in the Office of the President, to deal swiftly with complaints of all forms of discrimination, victimization and corruption, and to recommend appropriate measures for those found guilty. That agency should have, at least, one senior member of the PPP.

10. The PNC and PPP should both abstain from berating and vilifying each other at public meetings and through the

media and instead hold joint conferences and symposia and utilize other forums to pronounce on matters of national development.

That document was never formally discussed. Indeed, it met its own demise with the death of President Burnham.

Forbes Burnham

|5|

THE END OF DIALOGUE

The accession of Mr. Hugh Desmond Hoyte to the Presidency of the Republic introduced a critical determinant in the political situation of the country and the internal dynamics of the People's National Congress. From the beginning of his tenure, he attached fundamental importance to the national economy and conceived of the period of his stewardship to the nation as the "economic phase of our independence." It was clear to him, as he must have understood for some time that Guyana was, unjustifiably, being promoted as a surrogate of the USSR and had become a victim of Cold War politics. He, therefore, sought to reshape Guyana's political, economic and ideological policies, return the country to the mainstream of hemispheric politics, and, consequently, liberate it from the shackles of poverty and despair.

President Hoyte, like the Founder-Leader, as the late President Burnham is now referred to, was, and always has been, fiercely independent and strongly nationalist in outlook. They were more steeped in pragmatism rather than orthodoxy. Theirs was no great admiration of the Soviet bureaucratic system of Government or its rigid ideological precepts. The tenets of 'democratic centralism,' 'the dictatorship of the proletariat,' and 'proletarian internationalism,' for example, held out little or no appeal to them.[80] But for President Hoyte, it would seem that his great difficulty at that early stage of his presidency was how to reconcile his own perceptions of national development – which, at that historical period, veered sharply away from President Burnham's – with that of Dr. Jagan's continuing avowal of communism and his self-appointed position as the USSR's spokesman in the Caribbean.

At the same time, he had no great admiration either for Mrs. Janet Jagan, who continued to exert tremendous influence and power in the PPP. If it did seriously cross his mind, his dilemma would have been how to have a formal partnership with the PPP whose ideological and political positions were the exact opposite of his.

President Hoyte joined the People's National Congress in mid-sixties and was appointed a Minister of Government in 1968. Unlike his predecessor, he had never been a member of the People's Progressive Party, nor was he associated with the PPP in any way at all. Both as one time Minister of Home Affairs under President Burnham's Administration and as Head of State and, therefore, Head of National Security, he was not unaware of the seamier side of the politics of the PPP. On all counts he was on the opposite side of the Party's leadership.

The members of the PNC Working Group knew all of these things and the foremost question, therefore, which engaged their minds - and rightly so - was whether President Hoyte intended to perpetuate the Burnhamite tradition of accommodating the PPP or to go it without the PPP, stamping his unique style of leadership and management on the nation which destiny had placed under his authority and power.

Subsequent to the PNC's Biennial Congress, Mr. McDavid, in early October 1985, advised the Working Group that Dr. Reid had been in consultation with President

Hoyte, and the President suggested that the unity talks should be pursued with the People's Progressive Party. In an atmosphere overshadowed by the death of the former PNC Leader but defined by the powerful personality of the incumbent President, the Working Group re-commenced the process with a measure of uncertainty, since Mr. Hoyte neither meet formally with the members nor indicated that he wished to do so.

On October 15, 1985, President Hoyte departed Guyana for The Bahamas to participate in a Meeting of the Commonwealth Heads of Government that was being held from October 16-22, 1985. After the Commonwealth Summit, he was scheduled to visit New York from October 23 through 28, 1985.

On October 18, 1985, the PNC side met with its PPP counterpart rather suddenly, at the former's insistence, in the Committee Room of the National Assembly shortly after lunch. It was a Special Meeting convened on the instruction of the President before he left Georgetown for Nassau. It lasted for fifteen minutes.

In explaining the purpose of the meeting, Mr. Chandisingh observed that the PPP had breached the principle of confidentiality of the dialogue, and he alluded to an article published in the Sunday Mirror of October 6, 1985, under the banner headline of **Straight Talk by Cheddi Jagan**, which purported to commit the said breach. Exhibiting the offending newspaper article, he submitted that if the PPP should go public unilaterally every time on matters relating to the dialogue, the previous meeting would have wasted its time in establishing that principle.

Somewhat confused, the PPP spokesman, Mr. Feroze Mohamed, confessed that he was on leave from his job and that he did not see that particular publication of the Sunday Mirror. He, however, queried whether that article directly constituted a breach of the principle of confidentiality, and wondered if in future any political matter raised by Dr. Jagan in the public domain would be construed by the PNC as being related to the Inter-Party talks. He hoped that the claim of breach of confidentiality on the part of the PNC was not a disguised method of muzzling the PPP and Dr. Jagan.

Mr. Chandisingh contended that, in the opinion of the People's National Congress, Dr. Jagan's article did violate an important agreement reached by the two sides, and remarked that any further infraction could hardly redound to the good of the unity talks.

He re-emphasized that as far as he knew because no contrary instructions were issued to him, the PNC was genuinely interested in the successful outcome of the dialogue and enjoined the PPP to subscribe scrupulously to the decisions adopted at meetings. In concluding the session, Mr. Chandisingh informed the PPP representatives that arrangements for future meetings would be finalized in the manner previously agreed to.

On October 20, 1985, Mr. McDavid assembled the Working Group and informed its members that Dr. Reid had instructed that they should re-visit the document titled, *Some Tentative Proposal for the Formation of a United Fatherland Front of Guyana,* and that they should be in readiness to meet with the full Central Executive Committee so as to dilate on its contents when the President returned from his official business abroad.

The end of dialogue

The Working Group labored late many nights discussing, among other things, tactics and strategies relating to the upcoming presentation of the case to the Central Executive Committee. On the suggestion from Dr. Reid the title of the document was changed to *"Some Tentative Proposals for the Formation of a United Democratic Front."* Minor changes were made to the substantive document. The focus was more fundamental. Members of the Working Group were expected to explain to the Central Executive Committee how the power sharing paradigm was to be effected in practice and what would be some of the implications for the Party and Government.

On the afternoon of October 28, 1985, the Central Executive Committee of the People's National Congress convened at the Presidential Secretariat to discuss the new document. President Hoyte had just returned to Guyana some hours before. Bringing the meeting to order, Dr. Reid, Chairman of the Central Executive Committee, explained its purpose and called on President Hoyte to make the opening remarks. Looking at the document before him for the first time, he inquired who authorized its drafting, who was the author, and similar searching questions. It befell Mr. McDavid to explain the role of the Working Group and to accept full responsibility for its operations. He explained the background to its formation, the assignments that it had completed, and its preparedness to carry out the Central Executive Committee's directions.

Surprisingly, as the meeting progressed, the members of the Working Group came under sharp criticisms from the Party Leader. A few members of the Central Executive Committee also expressed their displeasure at the Group's seeming autonomy and its *modus operandi* and insinuated that it should be revamped.

In his final summation, President Hoyte rejected the document that was before him. He declared that, as Party Leader and President, **he** needed to give direction on the policies that the Party and Government would embark upon and not simply rubber-stamp those that had been hastily put before him. He said that the Party and Government needed to act as a cohesive body and not be perceived as engaging in factionalism in pursuit of old ideological affinities, the relevance of which had become questionable.

The President submitted that new circumstances had dictated new tactics and that the Party and Government had to rise to the occasion or else they would become anachronistic. He then gave directions for the Central Executive Committee to undertake the full burden of discharging the responsibilities associated with the unity talks, and instructed Mr. McDavid to meet with the PPP the following day in order wind up his discussions and to open the way for his successors to take over.

On October 29, 1985, at 5:00 p.m. the final meeting of the Inter-Party Preparatory Committee took place in the Committee Room of the National Assembly. In a rather strange way, the cycle of meetings ended where it all began a few short months ago. Mr. McDavid was the lone member from the PNC side. Mr. Chandisingh was unavoidably absent. Representing the PPP were Mr. Feroze Mohamed and Mr. Reepu Daman Persaud, Member of Parliament.

Mr. McDavid informed the PPP team that that meeting was likely to be his last with them since the PNC Central Executive Committee had assumed direct responsibility for the dialogue and might appoint other capable persons to conduct the negotiations. He held the view that the upcoming General Elections would not be an impediment to the talks since, as far as he understood it, the Central Executive Committee wanted a commitment from the PPP to proceed as rapidly as possible in that direction.

Mr. Mohamed inquired if the PNC anticipated a political solution before the elections and Mr. McDavid explained that the type of cooperation that the PNC envisaged would call for in-depth deliberations, and that was likely to take a longer time than was foreseen at that moment. He assumed that should the work move swiftly all things would be possible.

The meeting resolved that in order to shift the dialogue into a more productive mode the two sides should strive to develop an agenda that would result in positive action. In this regard, Mr. Mohamed said that the PPP would be willing to prepare a draft for consideration.

Finally, it was decided that a Press Release would be crafted and submitted to the PPP for approval.

But a silent, subdued pessimism overshadowed that meeting. It was presumed that the PPP representatives had some knowledge of what had transpired at the Presidential Secretariat. They probably perceived, also, that the latter round of meetings thus far lacked coherence and authoritative direction, at least, after the first meeting. Like Dr. Jagan, they most likely thought that under the new PNC leadership the unity talks had moved from solid ground to shifting sands.

After the official discussions, Mr. McDavid, Mr. Mohamed and I stood in the balcony of Parliament Building and spent some time talking about more personal matters and, of course, the future of Guyana. We separated with the hope that both sides would remain in touch with each other at the personal level.

And so, there was neither ceremonial flourish, dramatic displays nor acrimonious exchanges to signal the end of the dialogue. Just a little over eighty days after the sad passing of the Founder-Leader, the Burnham Initiative also died. Shortly afterwards, Mr. McDavid was relieved of his post as Chief Political Adviser to the President and appointed Guyana's Ambassador to Zambia. I was elevated to acting Chief Political Advisor to the President and Head of the Political Division. The Working Group simply faded into the sunset.

Inevitably, the reasons for the failure of the dialogue to fructify have to be addressed – even on a preliminary basis. In the absence of an official statement from President Hoyte and the Central Executive Committee some sort of tentative examination has to suffice, at least, for the time being. But in passing, it is to be noted that I had several times tried to engage him in this matter, to have him express a personal view. He always demurred.

In the first place, President Hoyte appeared not to be overly sanguine about the dialogue, in spite of his remarks at the PNC Sixth Biennial Congress. According to some high level members of the PNC, he was "emotionally anti-PPP" and as early as in 1976, he had opposed any alliance with Dr. Jagan and Mrs. Jagan.[81]

As the evidence indicates, historically, he demonstrated a preference for multilateral consensus instead of appealing to bilateral solidarity. Any arrangement, which involved only the PNC and the PPP, would hardly seem acceptable to him unless it was absolutely and completely necessary. Even then,

The end of dialogue

he would seek to involve other actors on the political scene – political parties, trade unions, and civic bodies. His strenuous advocacy and application of the principle of inclusion, and his stated recognition of the reality that he was the President of the entire nation and not segments of its populace, would not allow him to alienate any section from participating in the reconstruction of Guyana. Indeed, early in 1991, acting on an approved Motion sponsored by the Working People's Alliance (WPA) in the National Assembly, President Hoyte launched a National Dialogue project, for which he named me National Coordinator.[82]

That effort consulted with political parties, trade unions, religious organizations, and a large number of civic groups on how Guyana should advance into the new millennium. Unfortunately, for the country, that project met a premature end due to several intervening factors and, consequently, did not achieve its goals.

Rather strangely, Mr. Hoyte, time and again, demonstrated a keen disposition to accommodating the leadership of the Working People's Alliance – Dr. Rupert Roopnarine, Dr. Clive Thomas, Dr. Joshua Ramsammy and others in the WPA rather than with the PPP leadership.[83] This was fairly obvious to me and other senior advisors at the Office of the President. He liked and respected their brilliance. He believed that they were genuine patriots. It was in this context that the proposition that Guyana's highest National Award, the Order of the Excellence, be given to Dr. Walter Rodney on the occasion of the 150th Anniversary of the Abolition of Slavery in Guyana was discussed informally with him by his senior advisers quite a few times.

Secondly, President Hoyte's perceptions of national development and constructing a modern nation-state were diametrically opposite to the convictions of the PPP General Secretary. On his accession to the Presidency, he clearly acknowledged the changing temper of the times and sought to down play the ideological and political imperatives, which had transformed Guyana into a flashpoint of tension in the hemisphere. He concentrated on the economic dimension of development employing the free market mechanism in which the private sector was ascribed the leading role in the economy. At the same time, he began to focus on re-integrating Guyana in the mainstream of hemispheric politics.

President Hoyte's early overtures to the West even before he assumed the Presidency, his conciliatory address on the occasion of American Independence Day on July 4, 1985,[84] his re-building of cordial relations with Washington, and his efforts to seek financial support from the Bretton Woods institutions to enhance Guyana's development, among other things, led Dr. Jagan to bitterly attack him, describing him as a 'rightist' and 'opportunist.'[85] And so, while the PPP General Secretary was engaged in an unproductive exercise of labeling President Hoyte a capitalist, he was, at the same time, unrelentingly reinforcing his credentials as a Marxist-Leninist theoretician, strenuously advocating the building of socialism in Guyana and promoting closer ties with the Soviet Union and the world socialist community.

Thirdly, President Hoyte's conception of how Guyana's foreign policy should be framed was obviously in deep contradiction to Dr. Jagan's oft-expressed asseverations on that critical issue. Mr. Hoyte, like President Burnham, saw Guyana's destiny as being inextricably linked to the Caribbean Community and the Americas. He sought to have Guyana play a leading role in CARICOM, the Economic Commission of Latin America and the Caribbean (ECLAC), the Amazonian Pact, and the Organization of American States (OAS), among other regional institutions. At the wider international level, he emphasized Guyana's role in the Non Aligned Movement, the Commonwealth of Nations, and the United Nations. Dr. Jagan, at that time, however, wanted Guyana to conduct its internal and international relations in order to be accepted as part of the world socialist community headed by the USSR. In those days, the PPP General Secretary openly, publicly and repeatedly condemned 'US imperialism' as the scourge of humanity, and the PPP continued to maintain strong fraternal bonds with communist and workers parties, the World Federation of Trade Unions (WFTU), the World Federation of Democratic Youth (WFDY), the International Union of Students (IUS), and the International Organization of Journalists (IOJ), among other communist front organizations.

Fourthly, the influence of the United States on political developments in the country must be taken into consideration. The death of President Burnham made it easier and, in a way, more comfortable for Washington to undertake a rapprochement with the new People's National Congress Administration, given the ideological and political positions of President Hoyte, who had developed close relations with US Ambassadors Clint Lauderdale and Theresa Tull, as well as, Mr. Elliot Abrams, Assistant Secretary of State for Inter-American Affairs. During the early days of the Hoyte Administration, the United States showed no inclination to work with the PPP which continued with its strong pro-Soviet, pro-communist positions. This clearly strengthened Mr. Hoyte's position in avoiding the building of a working relationship with Dr. Jagan and the PPP. He believed that in seeking to constructively engage the PPP leadership in the process of national development that effort would most likely become ensnared in sterile ideological debates and would, therefore, hamstring his thrust toward economic reconstruction so badly needed at that time.

President Hoyte initiated the move away from socialism both internally and externally. In his own mind, he had abandoned the socialist agenda for Guyana. And so, subsequent to the demise of the Burnham-inspired dialogue, he proceeded on a systematic basis to weed out whatever socialist manifestations remained at large in the PNC. In this regard, he removed leftist elements of the Party and the Government from positions of influence and brought in technocrats who were more positively pre-disposed to the United States; he disbanded the Guyana Committee for Solidarity and Peace and allowed the Friendship Societies affiliated to the GCSP to fall by the wayside; he closed down the Cuffy Ideological Institute, the PNC's ideological training school, and directed that ideological training in Cuba and the Soviet Union be brought to an end, among other things.[85]

At the international level, Mr. Hoyte instructed that the GCSP sever its relations, prior to its disbandment, with the World Peace Council and, generally, de-emphasized relations with the socialist countries at both the Party and State levels. Military contacts with socialist countries were also terminated. In any case, his dealings with the Eastern European socialist governments, long before he became President, were frosty, to say the least.

Finally, there was the subjective dimension. When President Hoyte assumed the Presidency of Guyana, the PPP leadership did not reach out to him, as Head of State in his own right. In his views they looked at him as a Burnham puppet. That struck a discordant note which he was quick to internalize. At the same time, the PPP kept up the pressure on the new PNC Administration, utilizing GAWU to wield the strike weapon with deadly impact on the national economy. Mr. Hoyte took this as a personal affront to his Presidency. In 1985 alone there were 712 strikes and, again, widespread arson which mysteriously but usually accompanied the strikes in the sugar industry. And when President Hoyte held official discussions with Dr. Jagan as Minority Leader, the atmosphere, although cordial, was tense and electric. I know. I was there. In other words, there was no political chemistry between the two. The PPP leadership had neither studied nor read President Hoyte correctly, it would seem. They merely fitted him in the mould of his predecessor which some have called the height of political naivety.

Whatever the realities were, all the evidence suggested that there was no common ground between President Hoyte and Dr. Jagan in terms of *Weltanschauung* or world outlook, ideological beliefs, political programs, and prescriptions for economic development. An ocean of differences separated them and the ship of dialogue, which attempted to chart those waters, foundered on the rocks of intransigence and irreconcilability.

One may legitimately ask: what were the reactions of the Soviet Union and Cuba in the light of the collapse of the dialogue, given the fact that they were virtual stakeholders in that project? As far as I know, their key officials seemed to accept the inevitable and not very familiar with Mr. Hoyte, they did not raise the subject with him. Indeed, when I officially visited Moscow in February 1986 as a Personal Envoy of President Hoyte, the Latin America and Caribbean Department of the Communist Party of the Soviet Union (CPSU) officials, Mr. Dimitry Mauravyov and his colleagues, were more pre-occupied with getting acquainted with Mr. Mikhail Gorbachev, the new General Secretary of the CPSU, rather than losing sleep over the internal politics of Guyana.

Likewise it was with Cuba. The matter was never discussed officially with the Communist Party of Cuba. In private, the Cuban Ambassador, Mr. Lazaro Cabesas, who was based in Guyana at that time, Mr. McDavid and I discussed it in more nostalgic terms. But even when I accompanied President Hoyte on a State Visit to Cuba in January 1989, the issue never came up officially or unofficially with the Cuban functionaries in the Department of the Americas of the CPC or in any of the private discussions at which I was present with President Fidel Castro himself. Indeed, Mr. Rashleigh Jackson and Mr. Jeffrey Thomas would be able to confirm this as they were also present at all the private and other meetings with Dr. Castro.[86]

President Burnham leaving a meeting with former British Prime Minister, Margaret Thatcher. In the center, is the late Dr. Cedric Grant who, at the time, was Guyana's High Commissioner to the Court of St. James.

Forbes Burnham

|6|

WHITHER GUYANA!

Guyana is a land of less than one million people. As it advances into the new millennium, the political and ethnic cleavages have become more conspicuous and would appear to have deepened. The unity, however fragile, which preceded the fragmentation of the national movement in the 1950's has proven evasive so far and, instead of showing signs of maturing as a nation, some sections of the Guyanese people seem to be solidifying their differences, whether perceived or real, rather than emphasizing their similarities forged from a kindred heritage. Today, after a change of the Hoyte Administration and, indeed, the removal of the People's National Congress from state power and with the People's Progressive Party in its fourteenth year in government, Guyana is described as "a failed state" in current political analysis and social science literature.

Rotberg has argued that failed states are tense, deeply conflicted and dangerous. He pointed out that two important indicators of state failure are the growth of criminal violence and when arms and drug trafficking become more common, and when ordinary police forces become paralyzed. He contended that nation-states fail because they can no longer deliver positive political goods to their people.[87]

Jean-Germain Gros has submitted that "states fail when public authorities are either unable or unwilling to carry out their end of what Hobbes long ago called the social contract, but which now includes more than maintaining the peace among society's many factions and interests."[88] It would seem that current socio-political and economic conditions are moving Guyana into the direction of state failure.

Between 1961 and 1984, several attempts were made to effectuate some form of harmonious working relationship between the two major parties, the People's National Congress and the People's Progressive Party, which, it was hoped, would help to reduce conflict, create a cohesive and stable political environment, foster development, and enhance the national weal. None ever came to fruition. Have the seeds of ethnic division, sown by the imperial overlords, been so well fertilized and in turn have taken such deep, pervasive roots that they are unlikely to be dislodged? Or has it been that subjective factors – power, personality, and prejudice – have become so ingrained in the psyche of the national leadership that the nation's vital interests have been subordinated to personal agendas?

The 1984-85 Burnham Initiative would seem to have had the potential for generating an acceptable *modus vivendi* that could have helped to end the self-imposed alienation, to a large extent, of sizeable segment of the population and involve them in the mainstream of nation building. The inevitable question comes to mind: Had President Burnham not met his sudden demise what would have been the sequel to this endeavor that he had inspired?

Naturally, there is no 'correct' answer. Really, there could hardly be any definitive, unerring prediction of what would have happened. Any response, however serious, would have to be located in the realm of studied speculation.

Based on objective, empirical evidence and also on subjective, introspective considerations, it would appear that the unity talks would have resulted in a type of political compact between the two Parties which would have greatly reduced the potential for ethnic conflict, promote greater cultural respect, stimulate economic growth, greatly diminish political acrimony and generate political solidarity.

President Burnham was not oblivious to the political and economic realities of the times. He was politically astute enough to realize that the People's Progressive Party wanted more than good intentions and subjective considerations on the part of the PNC's leadership in arriving at the point where it could consider power sharing. He, therefore, hoped that the PPP would notice and acknowledge more sincerely the measures that the PNC Government had initiated since 1970, and, as a sign of his seriousness, he undertook to address some other preponderant concerns that troubled the PPP leadership.

President Burnham placed great emphasis on raising the ideological consciousness of Party leaders and members. In keeping with his own convictions, which accorded with the position of the PPP leadership, he had already established the Cuffy Ideological Institute, which was similar to the PPP's Accabre College of Social Sciences that taught the basics of scientific socialism. But in addition to local training, he adopted a policy whereby Party cadres were being sent to the Nico Lopez Ideological Institute in Cuba, the Komsomol School in Moscow, and the Kivokoni College in Tanzania. And he went further. Ideological education formed part of the curriculum of the Cyril Potter College of Education and the Lilian Dewar College of Education, and was introduced to the senior levels of the Public Corporations.

At the same time, in the Guyana Defence Force, ideological education was given priority, as it was in the Guyana National Service. Apart from internal education, senior ranks of the Disciplined Services were exposed collectively to this type of training at the Cuffy Ideological Institute.

In harmony with President Burnham's considered policy of re-orienting Guyana's economic and trading relations, Guyana began to develop stronger linkages with the Soviet Union and the Eastern bloc. The PNC Administration made a formal application for membership to the Council of Mutual Economic Assistance (CMEA). In fact, that application was taken to the CMEA by Mr. Hoyte in his capacity as Vice-President, Economic Development. Guyana's bauxite was being sold to Moscow and the German Democratic Republic. The Guyana Airways Corporation and the Guyana Defence Force acquired Tupolev and Antonov aircrafts, respectively, from the Soviet Union. Government delegations were being sent to Romania, Bulgaria, and other socialist countries to examine various aspects of cooperation. Guyana and Cuba successfully negotiated large scale fishing agreements and were expanding their trading relations.

The Burnham Administration embarked on a massive program to have hundreds of eligible Guyanese secure professional and technical training in the socialist countries. Guyanese from all ethnic backgrounds and different religious persuasions were given this rare opportunity for educational advancement at no cost to themselves, for President Burnham recognized that capacity building was crucial to the country's development. In this context, the Political Division of the Office of the President and the Public Service Ministry cooperated vigorously with the aim of securing a rather ample amount of scholarships in all fields from the socialist countries. I was the Office of the President liaison with the Public Service Ministry in this undertaking.

Mr. Fitz Alert, former Chief Training Officer, Public Service Ministry, and Dr. Roger Luncheon, currently Head of the Presidential Secretariat and political spokesman of the PPP/C Government, were sent on an extensive tour of Eastern Europe in this regard. Indeed, hundreds of scholarships were later offered to Guyanese students for undergraduate and postgraduate training. Cuba and the Soviet Union, in particular, began training a very large number of Guyanese students in the fields of medicine, dentistry, veterinary science and engineering, among other disciplines that were considered vital for national development. Additionally, more and more post-graduate scholarships were being taken up by Guyanese scholars and professionals at the University of the West Indies (UWI) - all of which were fully paid for by the Burnham Government.

In terms of international relations, the Burnham Administration pursued a foreign policy that was more akin to the positions adopted by the socialist countries, and played a pivotal role in the Non-Aligned Movement, championing with great vigor the cause of the Liberation Movements of Asia, Africa, and Latin America. At the same time, the PNC-inspired Guyana Council for Solidarity and Peace (GCSP) played a not insignificant role in the World Peace Council supporting those organizations and countries struggling against imperialism. Parallel to those developments, the PNC Biennial Congresses were graced by the presence of delegates and observers from communist and workers' parties the world over and, in turn, the PNC began attending congresses of communist and workers' parties as fraternal delegates and observers.

Meanwhile, gifts for the PPP coming from the Soviet Union, the German Democratic Republic, Bulgaria, Hungary and other socialist countries were readily uplifted from the Customs and Excise Department by the Party, without bureaucratic delays in keeping with a directive from the Office of the President. These included large amounts of newsprint for the New Guyana Company Limited, vehicles, motor-cycles, and public address equipment for the PPP and GAWU, and considerable supplies of books and other printed material for the Michael Forde Bookshop, among other things.

President Burnham was fully aware that the restriction on the importation of wheaten flour had aroused the feelings of being discriminated against among large sections of Guyanese. The myth is popular and is still being perpetuated as a reality that the restriction was effected because of ethnic prejudice. The real reason, of course, had to do with the ideological impulses of the Cold War and, more specifically, President Burnham's policies to pursue an independent path of development, which incensed the United States. He outlined the problem this way:

"In 1973, Guyana initiated negotiations with Cuba with a view to mutual trade. We were courteously and properly reminded by the American Government, through its Ambassador here, that if we were to trade with Cuba, the aid which we were receiving under…PL 480 would cease…

"We harbour no ill feelings against the United States of America. It's their aid programme. It's their right to prescribe the terms and conditions upon which aid will be given. We thanked them for the information, but we proceeded to trade with Cuba. And then the aid programme under PL 480 came to an end."[89]

After unsuccessful attempts to import flour from the socialist countries, he dispatched Mr. Elvin McDavid on a secret mission to Argentina, and Mr. Hubert Jack to Australia to explore the possibility of procuring wheat[90]. Like the socialist countries, they did not want to upset the United States Administration, which had virtually placed an embargo on wheat supplies to Guyana. He was in the process of attempting to secure such wheat supplies from third countries when he died.

President Burnham for sometime had commenced focusing on the matter of public corruption. In 1974, he had promulgated the Sophia Declaration, which, *inter alia,* purported to prevent corruption at the leadership level of the Party and Government. He, however, wanted to grapple with the issue in a more fundamental, systemic manner. He, therefore, tasked Brigadier-General David Granger from the Guyana Defense Force with the preparation of a Draft Policy Paper that would attempt to analyze the issue and make far-reaching recommendations that would seek to reduce the incidence of corruption and, and simultaneously, develop a culture of integrity and accountability in national life.

Finally, President Burnham, although he maintained close, personal contact with Dr. Jagan, always kept open an informal channel to the PPP through his old and trusted friend and colleague, Mr. Derek Jagan.[91]

Apart from those objective considerations, there seemed to be a subjective dimension to the whole notion of power sharing and political unity.

It would appear that the differences, which manifested in the fragmentation of the national movement in 1955, had become irrelevant to the two leaders after thirty years. L.F.S. Burnham and Cheddi Jagan had matured as men and professionals. They, who had hitherto fought each other, had found a common ideological home, in a way, at last; they had become members of the same socialist brotherhood; they had learned to speak a common language; they had earned the wrath of the same enemies. They now had to struggle for the realization of their common aspirations and labor for a common cause.

Dr. Cheddi (Joey) Jagan, Jr. has argued recently that the PPP Leader wanted a genuine working relationship with President Burnham. This is how he stated the argument:

"I can attest that President Cheddi (Jagan) wanted an end to this racial affliction affecting our beautiful country, he worried a lot about it and always considered working more closely with the PNC party to bring about a real rapprochement."[92]

Some leading members of the PPP's hierarchy have also mentioned that Dr. Jagan genuinely believed that "something positive" would have resulted from the Burnham Initiative.[93] It was clear to the two leaders that power sharing was an idea whose time had come. Indeed, the political moment had arrived for them to work out and settle the ground rules for national survival and development in an environment of peace and harmony. At that historical juncture, perhaps only those two leaders – given their historical relationship - had the magnanimity to reject political pettiness, put the political past firmly behind them and combine their individual talents and collective constituencies to move the Guyanese nation forward.

Today, with the death of Dr. Jagan and with Mrs. Janet Jagan the *de facto* leader of the Party, the PPP has, for all intent and purpose, repudiated Dr. Jagan's thesis that the winner does not take all. Power sharing is not currently on the PPP agenda and is not likely to be for a long time. In this regard, Mr. Moses Nagamootoo, Member of the PPP Central Committee and former Minister of Information,[94] has publicly declared that the PPP leadership should not have bluntly dismissed the PNC's position on power sharing which was recently adumbrated by the late President Hoyte.[95] He pointed out that the PPP leadership should stop fearing 'vendus.' He argued that "the time has come when we have to let go of the past. It is the past that is intruding in the present and blocking the way to the future… there are people around who cannot let the past go. The past wants revenge, like the ghost of Hamlet's father."[96]

Guyana now seems to be poised on the brink of an apparent unbridgeable abyss. With the PPP in its fourteenth year in government, crime and corruption have assumed alarming proportions, accusations of a State-sponsored "Death Squad"[79] have been rife, persistent allegations of ethnic and political discrimination have gained wide currency, the rate of migration has increased substantially and real economic development has been seriously curtailed.[98] The controversial 1997 General Elections which gave Mrs. Jagan the Executive Presidency were declared null and void by Justice Claudette Singh, and the wider issue of national governance continues to remain problematic.

Undoubtedly, to a large extent, Guyana is today politically and racially divided with political extremism seemingly in the ascendancy. And the grand vision of a unified Guyana, which inspired the Founding Fathers of our nation, L.F.S. Burnham and Cheddi Jagan, has become blurred with each passing day as antagonisms between the People's National Congress and the People's Progressive Party deepen, and societal contradictions widen.

Whither Guyana!

Forbes Burnham

Forbes Burnham

APPENDICES

APPENDIX 1

Dr. Ptolemy Reid's Letter to the Central Committee of the People's Progressive Party Proposing Formal Dialogue at the Leadership Level Between the People's National Congress and the People's Progressive Party.

1985-01-25
The Central Committee,
People's Progressive Party
Freedom House
41 Robb Street,
Georgetown.

Dear Comrades,

The Central Committee of the People's National Congress wishes to extend greetings to the Central Committee of the People's Progressive Party. We believe that as the struggle to preserve our independence and build socialism becomes more complex, new possibilities would arise for bolder initiatives and responses on the part of those who cherish these goals and aspirations.

The Central Committee of the People's National Congress, over the last two years, has been engaged in a constant process of examining and analyzing (i) the international environment, particularly the role of imperialism globally, and more specifically, its increased presence in the Caribbean, and (ii) the objective and sub-

jective conditions relative to the domestic economic and political situation.

In our analysis, we noted that imperialism has intensified its worldwide offensive. President Reagan's promise to "roll back the forces of communism" has precipitated a certain course of action which brought about increased tensions, endangered world peace, shattered early prospects for disarmament, and impelled the world towards the threshold of a nuclear catastrophe.

Further, we observed that imperialism continues to assume a predominant role in terms of economic hegemony in the Third World. In various forms and guises, and through a multiplicity of mechanisms and institutions, it persists in the plunder of poor countries — demonstrating no respite or indicating no intention of abandoning this policy and practice.

With regard to the Caribbean and Central America, our analysis concedes that imperialism has carved out an aggressive policy which includes military options in order to expurgate the "virus of Marxism" within the confines of its "fourth frontier." In this context, it has fragmented and divided the progressive movement in individual countries and buttressed right-wing regimes by means of sizeable military or paramilitary assistance. It undermined the unity of Caricom, engaged in economic and military aggression against sovereign states, and refused to recognize the Caribbean as a Zone of Peace. Above all, in blatant disregard of the norms of international behavior, and in direct challenge to the principles of the United Nations Charter and the Non-Aligned Movement, there took place a military intervention of the sovereign state of Grenada.

With reference to Guyana, we believe — as all empirical evidence show — that imperialism has operationalized more devious and subtle stratagems. These range from terrorist tactics (e.g. the Cubana murders, the bombing of the Guyana Consulate in Trinidad, the arming of mercenaries, etc.) to economic aggression and propaganda warfare. More recently, it has been organizing, mobilizing and financing local right-wing elements. Foreign intelligence services have infiltrated the WPA for the former's own purposes, and, at the same time, along with other western organizations, are providing material resources to the DLM in their campaign against both the People's National Congress and the People's Progressive Party.

Imperialism is vehemently opposed to the ideological positions of the People's Progressive Party. In similar manner, it shows a marked hostility to the People's National Congress for laying the foundations of socialism, its fraternal links with the world socialist community, its positive role in the Non-Aligned Movement and the United Nations. Given the present character of imperialism, and taking into account the fact that Guyana has effectively moved out of the orbit of capitalist relations, the guardians of international capital will exacerbate their attempts aimed at the demise of the ruling party and the emasculation of the People's Progressive Party.

We are certain that our analysis, in the main, corresponds with your interpretation. If you agree, it needs that both parties deal with the larger and more macrocosmic problem in an intelligent and mature way. Logically and inevitably, this implies dialogue at the leadership level with a view to hammering out on the anvil of give-and-take some form of political cooperation and unity. This becomes a crucial imperative if the asseverations of unity are to be infected with meaning and purpose, and, if also Guyana is to still pursue its anti-imperialist position and continue the process of building socialism.

In this context, the Central Executive Committee of the People's National Congress, by way of this letter, wishes to propose to the Central Committee of the People's Progressive Party that there should take place at a mutually agreed time and place follow-up talks at leadership level between the parties concerned - talks which were begun between the Chief Political Adviser and Clement Rohee, International Affairs Secretary of the People's Progressive Party, on May 30, 1984, and continued with Dr. Jagan during September 25-30, 1984, at Critchlow Labour College on the occasion of the TUC Conference.

Our Party Leader, Cde. L.F.S. Burnham has publicly expressed the need for unity, thereby sensitizing the nation to this imperative; the Guyana Committee for Solidarity and Peace has begun dialogue with the Guyana Peace Council; the Party's official organ, the New Nation, has completely refrained from attacks on the People's Progressive Party, and our various political functionaries have been assisting your party in the solution of any bureaucratic problems arising from time to time in the agencies under their charge. Needless to say, we are committed to this direction.

This is an historic moment and a challenging time for us. The Guyanese working class and working people are hopeful for a better tomorrow and a just society. Let us as partners in the struggle for socialism lead them to that goal.

The People's National Congress extends the hand of friendship and unity to the People's Progressive Party.

History will judge this offer and your Party's response to it.

Cooperatively,
P.A. Reid,
Deputy Leader and Chairman of the Central
Executive Committee,
People's National Congress.

APPENDICES

APPENDIX 11

Dr. Ptolemy Reid's Letter to Dr. Cheddi Jagan's Response dated February 11, 1985, to the People's National Congress Central Executive Committee.

1985-03-14
Dr. Cheddi Jagan,
General Secretary,
People's Progressive Party
Freedom House,
41 Robb Street
Georgetown.

Dear Comrade,

I have been directed by the Central Executive Committee (CEC) of my Party to acknowledge receipt of your letter dated February 11, 1985, in response to our invitation to your Party to hold discussions on a structured Party-to-Party basis at leadership level.

My Central Executive Committee has noted your expressed intention to consult with your membership before giving an answer to its proposal, and it would hope that your consultations would enable you to respond suitably on this important national question.

With respect to your request to be meanwhile provided with "specific suggestions" for cooperation, it would appear to my Central Executive Committee that any suggestions for cooperation may be conveniently raised and discussed within the inter-party structures which it has proposed. As you know, the whole object of CEC's proposal to establish such inter-party structures was to provide machinery to enable either party to raise, discuss and process matters for cooperation.

Accordingly, my Central Executive Committee is prepared to proceed to the establishment of the Preparatory Committee in order to commence discussion immediately on modalities, procedural matters, and other issues relevant to the proposed formal dialogue at leadership level as soon as your Party wishes.

With kind regards.

Yours Cooperatively,

P.A. Reid,

Deputy Leader and Chairman of the

Central Executive Committee.

APPENDIX 111

Dr. Jagan's Letter to Dr. P.A. Reid Indicating the PPP's Position to Enter into Discussions with the PNC on a Formal Basis.

May 20, 1985

Dr. P.A. Reid,

Chairman of the

Central Executive Committee

People's National Congress

Sophia.

Dear Comrade,

Our letter of Feb. 11, 1985, indicated to you that we would respond to your invitation for our two Parties to be in "constructive dialogue." Having completed the necessary discussions and consultations, the Executive Committee of the People's Progressive Party wish to inform you that we are prepared to enter into discussions with you on a formal basis.

In your invitation letter to us, you mentioned that such talks should deal with the very general questions of national development, security and socialist construction. On this score, you should recall that we had earlier referred you to the proposals contained in our Programme, For A Socialist Guyana, our 21st Congress Report, Strengthen the Party, Defend the Masses, Liberate Guyana, and our publication, For A National Patriotic Front Government.

Our Executive Committee takes this opportunity to remind you that we are of the firm belief that the economic and social difficulties facing our country cannot be solved without a political solution. We are of the view that, at this stage of Guyana's development, a government of all left and democratic forces based on democracy, anti-imperialism and socialist orientation is necessary. Such a government, in addition to representing the interest of workers, farmers, intelligentsia, small businessmen, patriotic capitalists and so on should also work towards laying firm foundations – political, economic, ideological, institutional, social, cultural – for the eventual "socialist construction" in Guyana.

We are also of the considered view that talks between our two Parties should cover certain pressing matters which require attention and urgent resolution.

Important among these are:

Ensuring democracy at the political, social and industrial levels and the people's fullest involvement in decision making. This would include official recognition of the genuine and democratic economic and social organizations of the people and respect for the constitutional rights of the democratically organized and run political organizations. Special attention should be paid to free and fair elections at the national, regional and local levels, and should include those re-

lated issues which our Party recently took up with Prime Minister Desmond Hoyte.

The need immediately to set up a Government/Opposition committee to examine the entire range of importation and distribution of goods and to put in place a system for the fair distribution of such goods.

Taking all practical measures to curb the lowering of the people's living standards and the deterioration of social services, whilst offering adequate wages and salaries and eliminating extravagance and all forms of discrimination and corruption in our society.

Safeguarding and defending our national sovereignty, independence and territorial integrity by, among other measures, expanding the People's Militia into every town, village and community.

Deepening Guyana's anti-imperialist policy and establishing the closest relations with the socialist community both for economic and social development and for defence of our political independence. From the socialist community, assistance should be requested for the establishment of a Central Planning Commission for the planned proportional development of the economy and the pursuit of ideological education in various educational institutions in Guyana.

We look forward to your ready agreement that the above-mentioned specific proposals be given the necessary emphasis they require in the Party-to-Party talks.

We also consider it necessary to draw attention to certain unfortunate developments since receiving you invitation letter.

We refer particularly to the disruption of PPP meetings at Cove and John and Bachelor's Adventure on February 18, 1985, and the seizure of our public address system; the uncalled for searches carried out on the premises of several PPP members and leaders; the disruption of the Annual General Meeting of the Guyana Council of Churches; the splitting of the trade union movement on May Day;

and a Bill introduced in Parliament to re-enact Part 11 of the National Security Act, which provides for preventive detention and violates the Rule of law. These do not create a favourable and suitable climate for the attainment of national unity and national development. We urge you to take steps which will create such a political climate.

Finally, we wish to suggest that a Committee made up of two members from each of our parties meet, at a mutually agreed time and place, to work out the technical aspects related to these talks.

Yours sincerely,
Cheddi Jagan,
General Secretary,
People's Progressive Party.

APPENDIX 1V

Press Statement Issued by the Office of the President on May 24, 1985, on the PPP's Response the PNC's Proposal for Constructive Dialogue.

The Minority People's Progressive Party today announced that it has responded to the PNC's call for "constructive dialogue" on a structured Party-to-Party basis at leadership level.

This latest response was made to the Central Executive Committee of the People's National Congress in a letter from Dr. Cheddi Jagan dated May 20, 1985.

In this letter, the PPP General Secretary explained that "having completed the necessary discussions and consultations, the Executive Committee of the People's Progressive Party wish to inform you that we are prepared to enter into discussions with you on a formal basis."

He went on to allude to "certain pressing matters" which he indicated would be raised by the PPP in the course of the proposed talks. The PPP General Secretary also drew attention to "certain unfortunate developments since receiving your letter of invitation."

Dr. Jagan finally concurred with a previous proposal made by the PNC's Central Executive Committee to have small preparatory team from both sides meet "at a mutually agreed time and place" to settle the modalities related to the talks.

APPENDIX V

Dr. P.A. Reid's Response to Dr. Cheddi Jagan's Letter of May 20, 1985.

1985-05-31
Dr. Cheddi Jagan,
General Secretary,
People's Progressive Party
Freedom house,
41 Robb Street,
Georgetown.

Dear Comrade,

Thank you for your letter of 20th May, 1985, in which you advised that your Executive Committee wished to inform me that your Party was prepared to enter into discussions with ours on a formal basis pursuant to our invitation for our two parties to be engaged in constructive dialogue.

We have noted the various matters which you feel should be covered by the proposed talks. Without prejudging the relevance, admissibility or exclusivity of issues sought to be raised, we feel that it would be more advantageous to both sides to leave to the Preparatory Committee any matter that would properly be the subject of the inter-party talks.

As regards the several allegations made in the penultimate paragraph of you letter, we do not believe you expected, and do not ourselves consider it appropriate to offer, a response at this stage and would confine ourselves to saying that our position on these matters is well known and, if necessary, can be further ventilated in the course of the talks.

Finally, although my Party would have been inclined to suggest that each side should be represented by three members on the Preparatory Committee, we accept your suggestion that the number of members should be two on each side. Our members will be Cde. Ranji Chandisingh, General Secretary, and Cde. Elvin McDavid, Member of the Central Executive Committee. We await your intimation.

If you will be good enough to let us know the names of your members, our Cde. Halim Majeed, Member of General Council of our Party, will be available to discuss with anyone you may designate, the time and place of meetings of the Preparatory Committee.

With kind regards.

Yours cooperatively,

P.A. Reid,

Deputy Leader and Chairman of the

Central Executive Committee.

APPENDIX V1

The PPP's Proposal on the Composition of the Political-Security Sub-committee and Socio-Economic Sub-committee and their Terms of Reference.

The Political-Security and Socio-Economic Subcommittees:

Composition:

1. *There shall be established two (2) Sub-committees.*

2. *Each Sub-committee will comprise six (6) persons with three (3) persons representing each side.*

3. *Both sides, after consultation, will incorporate on a temporary basis, such other persons who may be necessary to work in the corresponding Sub-committee from time to time. These persons will be called upon to deal with specific matters.*

4. One Sub-committee shall be called the Political-Security Sub-committee while the other shall be called the Socio-Economic Sub-committee.

5. Each Sub-committee shall discuss the topics assigned to it by the first meeting of the Inter-Party Commission.

6. Should differences arise on a given matter within a particular Sub-committee, the representatives in the Sub-committee shall refer such matter(s) to a higher body of their respective Parties with a view to resolving them.

7. The Sub-committees shall recommend matters agreed upon to the Inter-Party Commission for final approval.

Terms of Reference:

The Political-Security and Socio-Economic Sub-committees are mandated by the Inter-Party Commission to elaborate, collectively, a set of policies, the implementation of which, should contribute decisively to:

1. Uplifting the well being of the Guyanese people, the working people in particular.

2. The bringing about of the democratization of economic, social and political life of the country.

3. Increasing production and productivity.

4. Ensuring the protection of the country's territorial integrity and national sovereignty.

APPENDIX V11

The PPP's Proposal on the Inter-Party Commission and its Terms of Reference:

APPENDIX V11

The PPP's Proposal on the Inter-Party Commission and its Terms of Refernce:

Composition and Functions:

1. There shall be established an Inter-Party Commission.

2. The Inter-Party Commission shall be the highest expression of the Party-to-Party talks.

3. The Inter-Party Commission shall comprise ten (10) persons with five (5) persons coming from both sides.

4. The first Inter-Party Commission meeting shall mark the formal opening of the talks between the PPP and the PPP.

5. The first meeting of the Inter-Party Commission shall endorse the modalities, the terms of reference and guiding principles of the Inter-Party Commission and the Sub-committees.

6. The first meeting of the Inter-Party Commission shall agree on the topics for discussion in the Sub-committees.

7. The first meeting of the Inter-Party Commission shall provide the opportunity for the two sides to give a general assessment of the international, regional and local situations, the purpose of which shall be to identify positions on which the two sides agree and/or disagree.

8. The Inter-Party Commission shall issue mutually agreed to Press Releases from time to time, preferably after each meeting.

9. The Inter-Party Commission shall endorse the recommendations submitted from time to time by the Sub-committees.

Terms of Reference:

1. The Inter-Party Commission shall elaborate and lay down the general guidelines under which the Sub-committees shall operate.

APPENDICES

2. *The Inter-Party Commission will have the responsibility of synthesizing all recommendations coming from the Sub-committees with the aim of putting together a common programme which may serve as a basis for the realization of a political solution democratic in content for Guyana.*

APPENDIX VIII
SOME TENTATIVE PROPOSALS FOR THE FORMATION OF A UNITED FATHERLAND FRONT OF GUYANA.
A FIRST DRAFT FOR DISCUSSION

INTRODUCTION

During some stage in the process of socialist construction, or in times of crises which have originated as a result of internal and or external factors, it has been found necessary to unite the masses of people around a Fatherland Front. This has been the experience of many countries, which have built, and are continuing to build socialism.

The broad unity of the masses tends to guarantee the persistence of the Revolution, allows for the strengthening of the revolutionary process, and creates a powerful link between the people and the vanguard party.

In Guyana, the People's National Congress has been successful in winning and maintaining state power, achieving political independence, ushering in republicanism, and setting the stage for socialist transformation. However, given the present difficult internal and external situation, and contemporary geo-political realities, it is believed that a broad unity of all patriotic forces would have the potential of consolidating the revolutionary process, and advancing the struggle against imperialism and domestic reaction.

It is, therefore, suggested that consideration be given to the formation of a United Fatherland Front as a matter of priority.

SOME IMPERATIVES FOR THE FORMATION OF A FRONT

1. Imperialism has become stronger in the context of the Caribbean and Central America, and it has demonstrated in clear and unambiguous terms its aggressive nature. While it dispatched Michael Manley (and subsequently Milton Cato and George Price) through the electoral process, it has not flinched from exercising a military option in the case of Grenada. Of course, it needs to be reiterated that the Grenadian situation was made possible by internal events, which divided the then government and the people.

2. Imperialism has been supporting the ultra-right and ultra-left groups in Guyana, which exploit our difficult economic situation and which pander to ethnic and religious considerations. Naturally, this support is biased in favor of the overthrow of the ruling party.

3. The People's National Congress, as the nation's vanguard, is desirous of forging the broadest possible unity of all anti-imperialist and patriotic forces in order to further unify the nation, and deepen the present process of socialist transformation. The Party must, therefore, take the more practical initiatives, which would lead to the creation of a Front.

4. A United Fatherland Front would also place our present revolutionary process on a solid foundation, and act as the catalyst for increasing material production and productivity, and guaranteeing the all-round defense of the nation.

5. A United Fatherland Front would deflect and defuse attacks on the ruling party and could very well have the potential of giving increased momentum to the state of economic relations between Guyana and the world socialist community.

APPENDICES

DEFINITION AND COMPOSITION OF THE FRONT

The United Fatherland Front is to be perceived as the main (as separate and distinct from the leading) political organization in the country.

It is anticipated that the Front would comprise the three political parties as presently represented in Parliament. What is proposed for consideration also is the inclusion of mass organizations, the trade union movement, the umbrella church organization, etc.

AIMS AND OBJECTIVES

The Front would have the following main objectives:

1. To consciously work for the maintenance and preservation of Guyana's sovereignty, independence, and territorial integrity;

2. To facilitate and advance Guyana's independent path to political, economic, and social development;

3. To deepen the unity between the Guyanese working class and other working people;

4. To advise Government on policy directions from time to time.

ORGANIZATION OF THE FRONT

It is proposed that the Front should be organized as follows:

1. The Central Committee

2. The Central Coordinating Committee

3. The Secretariat

4. Regional Committee

5. District Committees

Representation on all the above would be based on the present parliamentary seats in the National Assembly, namely, People's National Congress – 67 percent; the People's Progressive Party – 28 percent; United Force – 5 percent.

If the United Force does not wish to participate in the Front, then the PNC and PPP would have 70 percent and 30 percent respectively.

If it were decided to include mass organizations, churches and the trade union movement, then the composition of the various bodies of the Front would have to be more carefully considered.

The Central Committee, it is further proposed, should be headed by the main minority party, and the Secretariat by a Secretary-General from the ruling party. (This could be optional, however, to allow the Leader of the ruling party to head both the Front and the Government).

The Central Committee of the Front would be large in number, and would enunciate the political program of the Front. It would meet once every six months.

The Central Coordinating Committee would be smaller in relation to the Central Committee, and will meet once per quarter.

The Secretariat, under the Secretary-General, would be responsible for the day-to-day administration of the Front.

In any elections, including National Elections, the Front would put up a joint list to contest same.

The composition, in terms of actual numbers for the various Committees, would be agreed upon collectively by the political parties.

APPENDICES

ORGANIZATION OF THE GOVERNMENT

It is proposed that the new Government should be organized as follows:

- *National Assembly;*
- *Supreme Congress of the People;*
- *Council of State;*
- *Council of Ministers.*

The **National Assembly** *would be constituted on its present allotment of seats or any other negotiated settlement. It would meet once per quarter.*

The **Supreme Congress of the People** *would be an Advisory Body to Parliament. Seats would be allotted to the trade unions, mass organizations, the Chamber of Commerce and the churches, apart from the political parties. It may also include Vice-Presidents of the Republic. It would also meet once per quarter.*

The **Council of State** *is expected to be the most important structure of Government. It would comprise the President of the Republic, Vice-President, and other elected and nominated representatives. It would constitute the main decision making body of the Government. The Head of the Council of State will be the Head of State. It would meet fortnightly.*

The **Council of Ministers** *would implement the decisions of the Council of State and the National Assembly. It would be chaired by the Head of State or his nominee.*

CONSTITUTIONAL CHANGES

If the main proposals are agreed upon by those concerned, then a number of constitutional changes would be required.

CONCLUSION

As has been stated in the beginning, this Presentation is a first document of tentative ideas for discussions. It sets out the rationale for the organization of the Fatherland Front, and seeks to elaborate a basic format as to how the Front should be organized. Naturally, it has to be discussed exhaustively in order to reach the stage of a formal proposal, which would be submitted to the various interested parties.

This document is now submitted for examination and discussion.

Political Division,
Office of the President,
July 1985.

Forbes Burnham

NOTES

1. Fred Wills was a brilliant Guyanese Attorney-at-Law, who had a distinguished legal career. He attained the dignity of Senior Counsel (SC) and served as a Member of Parliament and Minister of Foreign Affairs under the Burnham Administration from 1975-1978, replacing Sir Shridath Ramphal.

2. Sir Shridath Ramphal was appointed Minister of State for External Affairs shortly after Guyana became independent in 1966. He also held the portfolio of Attorney General. He is generally regarded as the architect in the creation of Guyana's foreign policy during the early years of the Burnham Administration. He left the Guyana diplomatic service in 1975 and later served as Commonwealth Secretary-General for two terms. He is widely recognized as one of the leading Caribbean integrationists and is co-author of **Time for Action: A Blueprint for Caribbean Integration**.

3. Rashleigh Jackson literally grew up in Guyana's diplomatic service. He served as senior officer in the 1960's and was later appointed Permanent Secretary in the Ministry of Foreign Affairs. In 1972, he was appointed Guyana's Permanent Representative to the United Nations and was President of the UN Council for Namibia. He succeeded Fred Wills as Minister of Foreign Affairs in 1978 and served both the Burnham and Desmond Hoyte Administrations.

4. Bryn Pollard is an extraordinary legal draughtsman who served in the Chambers of the Attorney General of Guyana for many years. He was subsequently appointed as Legal Advisor in the Office of the Secretary General of the Caribbean Community (CARICOM). He is the recipient of both National and Regional Awards for his outstanding legal services in the region.

5. Keith Massiah is an eminent Guyanese jurist, serving with distinction in the legal profession. He spent many years in the judiciary serving as a High Court Justice, Justice of Appeal and finally, as Chancellor of the Judiciary. He was appointed later as Minister of Legal Affairs and Attorney General under the Desmond Hoyte Administration.

6. Keith Massiah, (Guyana) Stabroek News, December 15, 2002, Letter to the Editor titled, <u>Fred Wills was the brightest of our group</u>.

7. Shirley Patterson, <u>Biographical Sketch of the Prime Minister Mr. L.F.S. Burnham</u>, Unpublished, Undated Manuscript.

8. Dr. Cheddi Jagan studied dentistry at Howard University, Washington, DC, and North Western University in Chicago (1936-1943). He married Janet Rosenberg and returned to the then British Guiana where, in 1950, he established the Political Affairs Committee (PAC), the forerunner of the People's Progressive Party.

9. The Working People's Alliance (WPA) is more or less an amalgamation of a number of political groups, Ratoon, Movement Against Oppression, Indian People's Revolutionary Organization and ASCRIA. Some of the more promi-

nent members of the WPA were Eusi Kwayana, Dr. Clive Thomas, Dr. Walter Rodney, Moses Bhagwan, Dr. Rupert Roopnarine and Dr. Joshua Ramsammy. It was formed in 1979 and recently celebrated the 25th anniversary of its founding.

10. Cheddi Jagan, <u>The West on Trial: My Fight for Guyana's Freedom</u>, Hansib Caribbean, St. John's, Antigua, 1997, p. 97.

11. L.F.S. Burnham, <u>A Destiny To Mould, Selected Speeches</u>, London, Longman, Caribbean, 1970, pxviii.

12. The PPP Central Committee expelled Mr. Khemraj Ramjattan, Attorney-at-Law, from the People's Progressive Party on February 13, 2004, for being critical of Party policies.

13. Janet Jagan nee Rosenberg is an American by birth. She is of Romanian heritage and came into prominence in Guyana with the founding of the People's Progressive Party (PPP) in 1950. She has held many posts in the PPP: General Secretary, International Affairs Secretary, Trustee of the PPP, Editor of the Party's newspaper, **Mirror**, and a member of various committees of the Party. She served as a Minister of Government in the first PPP Administration (1953) and in subsequent PPP Administrations. After the death of President Cheddi Jagan in 1997, she assumed the Presidency in what has become a controversial affair. She remains a leading member of the PPP.

14. The United Democratic Party (UDP) was formed in the 1950's and contested the 1957 General Elections. Its principal leaders were Sir John Carter and W.O.R. Kendall.

It subsequently aligned itself with the People's National Congress (PNC).

15. United Force (UF) was formed early in 1961. Its leader was Peter D'Aguiar, well-known and successful entrepreneur. The UF coalesced with the PNC in 1964 and formed the new Government in which LFS Burnham became Prime Minister and Mr. D'Aguiar Minister of Finance.

16. Cheddi Jagan, West on Trial, op.cit p. 325.

17. *Ibid.* p. 362

18. L.F.S. Burnham, *op.cit* p. 67.

19. H.D. Hoyte, Republic Day Address Tuesday 22nd February, 2000, http://www.guyana_pnc.org/ MediaCentre

20. H.D. Hoyte, *Ibid.*

21. Guyana Graphic, February 23, 1969, Dr. Jagan calls for Feb. 23 as National Holiday.

22. Multilateral Schools were new secondary schools with a broad-based curriculum that included, among other things, agriculture and home economics.

23. The Black Bush Polder (Berbice) and Tapacuma (Essequibo) agricultural schemes had brought large areas of land under cultivation. Those schemes produced substantial quantities of rice, vegetables and ground provisions. The former was estimated to cost about US$ 44 million and benefited from a USAID loan of G$ 19 million. The latter was expected to bring 66,000 acres of land under cultivation and was undertaken under a 1977 World Bank loan of US$ 29 million.

Notes

24. Timehri International Airport was changed to the Cheddi Jagan International Airport after the PPP assumed the reigns of Government in 1992.

25. The other signatories to the Treaty of Chaguaramas, which was signed on July 4, 1973, were Prime Ministers Errol Barrow (Barbados), Michael Manley (Jamaica), and Dr. Eric Williams (Trinidad and Tobago). By Treaty revision, effective February 2002, the successor entity is now the Caribbean Community, including the CARICOM Single Market and Economy (CSME).

26. Rashleigh Jackson, <u>Non-intervention and Intervention: CARICOM in Action – Grenada 1979 and 1983</u>, Stabroek News, Sunday, September 1, 2002.

27. The term 'Non-Alignment' was coined by Jawaharlal Nehru in 1954 during a speech in Sri Lanka. The Non-Aligned Movement can be traced to the Bandung (Indonesia) Conference in 1955. Six years later, the first Conference, through the initiative of Josip Broz Tito of what was then Yugoslavia, was held. Other prominent leaders included, Gamal Abdel Nasser of Egypt, Kwame Nkrumah of Ghana, and President Sukarno of Indonesia.

28. The Latin American Economic System (SELA) is a regional intergovernmental organization that groups 26 Latin American and Caribbean countries. Its headquarters are in Caracas, Venezuela. SELA was established on 17 October 1975, by the Panama Convention.

29 The African Caribbean Pacific Group - the Cheddi Jagan Administration refused to support Mr. Greenidge's selection to the ACP although other CARICOM, Member States expressed complete solidarity with Mr. Greenidge.

30. Luis Posada Cariles is of Cuban origin and is a former CIA operative and an intelligence officer of the Venezuelan security services. He is connected to numerous assassination attempts on the life of President Fidel Castro and is implicated in the murders of other Cuban officials. Posada is currently wanted by Venezuela for escaping from prison in 1985 while awaiting a prosecutor's appeal of his second acquittal in the Cubana Airlines bombing, which killed all aboard. According to Eva Golinger, a Venezuelan-American Attorney, (www.venezuelanalysis.com) Posada is a fugitive from justice in Venezuela and an international terrorist, so defined by the Federal Bureau of Investigations (FBI), and therefore cannot be granted political asylum under U.S. law.

On Tuesday, May 17, 2005, Posada was detained by the US Department of Homeland Security. The move came shortly after Posada emerged from about two months in hiding in the Miami area. He was smuggled in to the United States through Mexico, according to media reports. Venezuela has recently approved a formal extradition request and Cuba has made numerous statements denouncing Posada as a terrorist and accusing the United States of double standards on the war on terror. The United States and Venezuela have an extradition treaty. Orlando Bosch was labeled a terrorist back in the 1970's by the FBI. He has been involved in a multitude of terrorist activities including the bombing of the Guyana Consulate in Trinidad and Tobago, the kidnapping of Cuban diplomatic officials in Argentina, the bombings of many Cuban diplomatic missions around the world, the murders of a number of Cuban diplomats, including Felix Garcia Rodriguez, a Cuban official at the United Nations in 1980. In 1987, he received a US Presidential pardon and now resides in the United States.

31. Generally, relations between Guyana and the United States were at low ebb in this period. They only improved substantially when President Burnham died in 1985 and President Desmond Hoyte assumed the Presidency after his death. In the course of his tenure, President Hoyte paid official visits to the United States and met with Presidents Ronald Reagan and George Bush, and other high level Administration officials. I accompanied him on those visits to the United States.

32. The Council for Mutual Economic Assistance (CMEA), sometimes referred to as COMECON, was an international organization active between 1956 and 1991 for the coordination of economic policy among socialist countries. It was formed in 1949 but a formal charter was not ratified until ten years later. The organization was disbanded in June 1991 following the changes in Eastern Europe.

33. This was compiled by looking at a number of World Bank documents during that period.

34. Discussions with Mr. Ronald Austin, former Deputy Chief Political Advisor to President Burnham and later Guyana's Ambassador to China, February 18, 2004.

35. Hugh Desmond Hoyte, We Can, We Must, We Will, Address by His Excellency Hugh Desmond Hoyte, S.C., Leader of the People's National Congress and President of the Cooperative Republic of Guyana, to the Sixth Biennial Congress of the People's National Congress at the Sophia

Convention Centre, August 19, 1985, Georgetown, Guyana, GNNL, pp. 2 -3.

36. These lines were taken from Alfred Tennyson's famous poem, "Ulysses."

37. The Kaieteur News then was a weekly newspaper published in Guyana by Mr. Glen Lall.

38. See Arthur M. Schlesinger's **A Thousand Days: John F. Kennedy in the White House**, Houghton Mifflin Company, 1965. The British described Dr. Jagan in these terms: "He is a confused thinker and his mind is clogged with ill-digested dogma derived from Marxist literature." (See Document 246, Kennedy Library, National Security Files, Countries Series, British Guiana, May 19-Aug.23, 1961. Secret).

39. The Declaration of Sophia was an important policy document of the People's National Congress setting out the Party's position on national development.

40. Mr. Ranji Chandisingh, then Deputy Leader of the PPP, and Mr. Feroze Mohamed, then First Secretary of the Progressive Youth Organization, also attended this meeting.

41. Private conversations with leading officials of the Americas Department of the Communist Party of Cuba in 1975 on the political situation in Guyana.

42. The (Guyana) Daily Chronicle, August 10, 1975.

43. The (Guyana) Sunday Chronicle, August 10, 1975.

44. *Ibid*

45. This was revealed on a television interview with Mr. Robert Corbin in April 2002 and in private discussions with the author. Mr. Corbin, of course, went into details of the talks with the author.

46. H.B. Jeffrey and Colin Baber, Guyana: Politics, Economics and Society, London, Frances Pinter Publishers, 1986, p. 112

47. In a private discussion with Mr. Zaheer Majeed in 1976 at his Belfield Residence, Mr. Burnham, in one of his more introspective moments, said, "Had Cheddi married a Guyanese, the history of Guyana would have certainly been different."

48. This information contained in this paragraph and the following three were revealed at several Tuesday afternoons' discussions at the poolside of the Vlissingence Road Residence of President Burnham (now Castellani House) with his senior advisers in 1983 and 1984.

49. Mr. Khemraj Ramjattan, former PPP Central Committee member, raised the matter of financial accountability in the PPP more contemporaneously during a meeting in New York on Sunday, April 11, 2004. See letter in Stabroek News dated April 18, 2004, captioned, Resolution at New York meeting calls for re-instatement of Ramjattan.

50. Eusi Kwayana's "Common Sense About Power Sharing" in (Guyana) Stabroek News, April 1, 2001.

51. Cheddi Jagan, op.cit. Chapter xv

52. Cheddi Jagan, op. cit. p. 429.

53. Cheddi Jagan, op. cit. p. 430

54. The Basic Principles of Relations Between the United States of America and the Union of Soviet Socialist Republics was signed on May 29, 1972 in Moscow. Among the things that were agreed to were (i) differences in ideology did not constitute obstacles to the principles of sovereignty, equality, non-interference in the internal affairs of states and mutual advantage; (ii) the USA and the USSR will negotiate and settle their differences by peaceful means; (iii) the two countries would do everything in their power so that conflicts or situations will not arise which would serve to increase international tension.

55. In his seventh annual message to Congress in 1823, President Monroe put European Powers on notice that the American region was off limits to European colonization and that any attempts to interfere with American lands would be considered a manifestation of an unfriendly disposition toward the United States. The Brezhnev Doctrine was articulated in 1968 after the Czechoslovakian Communist Party, under the leader Alexander Dubcek, attempted to introduce a number of reforms in the country. Warsaw Pact forces invaded Czechoslovakia and deposed Dubcek that year. It declared that no Soviet satellite state would be allowed to separate from the Eastern Bloc, headed by the USSR.

56. Thunder, Vol. 17, No. 3, Third Quarter, 1985, Political Resolution at the Twenty Second Congress of the People's Progressive Party, August 1985.

57. President Burnham also sought, at the same time, to maintain cordial relations with the United States. According

to Dr. Tyrone Ferguson in his book, **To Survive Sensibly or to Court Heroic Death: Management of Guyana's Political Economy 1965-85**, "a novel form of bilateral dialogue designed to achieve Burnham's expressed desire to improve relations with the United States" was initiated. It involved contacts at the United Nations between Guyana's Permanent Representative, Noel Sinclair, and the US Permanent Representative, Jeanne Kirkpatrick; in Washington between Guyana's Ambassador Cedric Grant and the US State Department; in Guyana between Ambassador Rudy Insanally and US Ambassador Clint Lauderdale.

58. While it was not evident at the time, the USSR had entered the stage of economic decline also.

59. The PPP called for a political solution. See (Guyana) Sunday Chronicle August 10, 1975, and the Political Resolution of the PPP Twenty Second Congress, August 1985.

60. Confidential Report from Mr. Patrick Denny to the Chief Political Adviser to the President dated December 5, 1984.

61. *Ibid.*

62. *Ibid.*

63. The Disciplined Services consisted of the Guyana Defence Force, the Guyana National Service, the Guyana Police Force, the Guyana Fire Service, the Guyana Prison Service and the Guyana People's Militia.

64. Dr. Ptolemy Reid served the Burnham Administration in various capacities, some of them being Minister of Home Affairs, Minister of Agriculture, Minister of National

Development, and Prime Minister. He was appointed Prime Minister in 1980 after the introduction of the new constitution promulgated that year.

65. Notes of the People's National Congress General Council Meeting, January 1985.

66. *Ibid*

67. See Appendix I for Dr. Reid's letter dated January 25, 1985.

68. This is the candid opinion of a leading PPP member who prefers not to be mentioned by name at this time. He pointed out to me that the PPP leadership was caught off guard by the letter from Dr. Reid.

69. See Appendix II for Dr. Reid's letter dated March 14, 1985.

70. See Appendix III for Dr. Jagan's letter dated May 20, 1985.

71. See Appendix IV for the full text of the Press Statement.,

72. See Appendix V for Dr. Reid's letter dated May 31, 1985.

73 Notes of the First Preparatory Meeting (taken from the author's personal collection of political documents).

74. *Ibid*

75. Appendix VIII for the full text of the document

76. Address by His Excellency Cde. H.D. Hoyte, S.C., Leader of the People's National's Congress and President of the Cooperative Republic of Guyana, to the Sixth Biennial Congress of the People's National Congress at Sophia Convention Centre – Monday August 19, 1985, pp 14 -15.

77. See Appendices VI and VII.

78. Mr. Elvin McDavid used this term when submitting the document to President Burnham.

79. The National Honors Committee had offered National Awards to leading PPP stalwarts such as the late Mr. Boysie Ramkarran, who declined acceptance because of the PPP policy at the time.

80. President Burnham, although he publicly expressed admiration for the Soviet Union, was never really enamored with its bureaucratic system – hence the advocacy of Cooperative Socialism – the attempt to find new, indigenous forms of organization, which aimed at diminishing and removing alienation. Also, he regarded Leninism as a peculiarity of the Russian situation and circumstances. It is to be noted that the PNC Government criticized the USSR invasion of Czechoslovakia in 1968. At the time, the PPP vigorously supported the Soviet position. Later, Dr. Jagan, in 1991, at the PPP 24th Congress, admitted that the PPP had made a mistake. In short, President Burnham was not the orthodox Marxist-Leninist.

81. Interviews with several high-ranking members of the Central Executive Committee of the People's National Congress who do not wish to be named at this time.

82. President Hoyte met formally with a delegation from the WPA at the Office of the President to discuss their ideas on National Dialogue.

83. When Sister Rowtie, a Catholic nun, and some WPA activists, were attacked in Albouystown during a protest march that she was leading, President Hoyte personally gave the Commissioner of Police orders, in my presence, to "arrest all and sundry" who were involved in the incident. And when the Police attempted to prevent a WPA-led march on the Kitty Railway road, President Hoyte instructed me to go on location and to inform the Police that they should not interfere with the marchers because the WPA had not broken the law.

84. Certain leading PNC members, on reviewing the Book, pointed out, in no uncertain terms, that these things were done with the concurrence of President Burnham.

85. Mr. Elvin McDavid, in an interview, mentioned that President Hoyte instructed him to "cease forthwith all anti-American rhetoric" shortly after President Burnham's death.

86. Ambassador Ronald Austin and then Head of the Presidential Secretariat, Mr. Cedric Joseph, also accompanied President Hoyte on the State Visit to Cuba and were present at several meetings with President Castro.

87. Robert Rotberg, The New Nature of Nation-State Failure, http://www.twq.com/02summer/rotberg.pdf

88. Jean-German Gros, 'Towards a taxonomy of failed states in the New World Order: decaying Somalia, Liberia, Rwanda and Haiti,' Third World Quarterly, Vol. 17, 3, p. 456.

89. See L.F.S. Burnham's Address for the Victims of the Cubana Air Disaster, October 17, 1976: Caribbean Yearbook of International Relations, pp. 574-580.

90. The Soviet Union itself had all along been short of wheat, which it was importing heavily from North America.

91. Mr. Derek Jagan, Attorney-at-Law, was the brother of Dr. Jagan and also a high-ranking member of the PPP.

92. Dr. Cheddi (Joey) Jagan's letter published in (Guyana) Stabroek News, Tuesday March 5, 2002.

93. Personal conversations with some leading PPP members who do not want to be identified at this time.

94. Mr. Nagamootoo has recently declared that he was "resigned" by the PPP since he has not submitted a formal letter of resignation to the party. See Guyana Stabroek News, Sunday, July 3, 2005, Nagamootoo denies resigning from the PPP Executive Committee - says Party resigned him.

95. On October 16, 2002, the People's National Congress/Reform published its views on power sharing.

96. See Selwyn Ryan, Why Power Sharing Won't Work, Trinidad Express, August 25, 2002.

97. The Government of Guyana has been widely accused of controlling a Death Squad. Media reports linked former Minister of Home Affairs to a well-known criminal, Axel Williams, and a group of underworld figures. He later officially resigned his portfolio. Under public pressure, President Jagdeo established a Commission of Inquiry which, subse-

quently, cleared Minister Gajraj of criminal wrong doing. He was re-appointed Minister of Home Affairs but, after the United States, Canada, the United Kingdom and Guyana's largest aid donor, the Inter-American Development Bank, expressed their displeasure, he was forced to quit his Governmental position. The Government appointed him High Commissioner to India which is the subject of another controversy

BIBLIOGRAPHY

BOOKS AND ARTICLES

Burnham, L.F.S., A Destiny to Mould, London, Longman Caribbean, 1970.

Burnham, L.F.S., Declaration of Sophia, Address by the Leader of the People's National Congress, at a Special Congress to mark the 10th Anniversary of the PNC in Government, Sophia, Georgetown, December 14, 1974.

Burnham, L.F.S., Address for the Victims of the Cubana Air Disaster, October 17, 1976, Caribbean Yearbook of International Relations.

Burnham, L.F.S., Economic Liberation Through Socialism, Leader's Address, 2nd Biennial Congress of the PNC, Sophia, Georgetown, August 12-20, 1977.

Burnham, L.F.S., Towards The People's Victory, Leader's Address, 3rd Biennial Congress of the PNC, August 22-26, 1979.

Burnham, L.F.S., Organize for Production and Defence, Address by the Leader of the People's National Congress, President Cde. L.F.S. Burnham, at the Fourth Biennial Congress of the People's National Congress at Sophia, Greater Georgetown, August 22-29, 1981.

Burnham, L.F.S., Will to Survive, Address by Cde. L.F.S. Burnham, Leader of the People's National Congress and President of the Cooperative Republic of Guyana at the Fifth Biennial Congress of the PNC, Sophia, Georgetown, August 14-21, 1983.

Ellis, Clarence and Phillips, Eric, Power Sharing for Racial Harmony, NOL

Ferguson, Tyrone, To Survive Sensibly or to Court Heroic Death: Management of Guyana's Political Economy, 1965-85, Georgetown, PACE, 1999.

Gros, Jean-Germain, Towards a taxonomy of failed states in the New World Order: decaying Somalia, Liberia, Rwanda and Haiti, Third World Quarterly, Vol. 17, 3, 1996.

Hinds, David, Race, Democracy, and Power Sharing, An Address delivered at the Walter Rodney Memorial Lecture, July 19, 2001, Tower Hotel, Georgetown, Guyana.

Horowitz, Donald, Ethnic Groups in Conflict, Berkley, University of California Press, 1985.

Hoyte, Hugh Desmond, We Can, We Must, We Will, Address by His Excellency H.D. Hoyte, S.C., Leader of the People's National Congress and President of the Cooperative Republic of Guyana to the Sixth Biennial Congress of the People's National Congress at the Sophia Convention Centre, August 19, 1985, Georgetown, Guyana National Printer Limited, 1985.

Hoyte, Hugh Desmond, Republic Day Address, Tuesday 22nd February, 2000, http://www.guyana-pnc.org/Media-Centre

Jackson, Rashleigh, Non-intervention and Intervention: CARICOM in Action – Grenada 1979 and 1983, Stabroek News, Sunday, September 1, 2002.

Jagan, Cheddi, The West on Trial: My Fight for Guyana's Freedom, St. John's Antigua, Hansib Caribbean, 1997.

Jagan, Cheddi, Address delivered to the 25th Anniversary Conference on behalf of the Central Committee of the People's Progressive Party by the General Secretary, August 3, 1975, Thunder, Vol. 7, No. 3, September-December, 1975.

Jagan, Cheddi, Report of the Central Committee of the PPP, Thunder. Vol. 8, No. 3, July-September, 1976.

Kwayana, Eusi, Common Sense about Power Sharing, Stabroek News, April 1, 2001.

Lamarchand, Rene, Patterns of State Collapse and Reconstruction in Central Africa: Reflections on the Crisis in the Great Lakes, Africa Spectrum, 32, 2, 1997.

Lijphart, Arend, Democracies in Plural Societies, a Comparative Exploration, New Haven, Yale University press, 1997.

Massiah, Keith, Fred Wills was the brightest of our group, Stabroek News, December 15, 2002.

Patterson, Shirley, Biographical Sketch of the Prime Minister Mr. L.F.S. Burnham, unpublished manuscript.

Ryan, Selwyn, Why power sharing won't work, Trinidad Express, August 25, 2002.

Ryan, Selwyn, Stability for a Ruling Party Worth Buying, Trinidad Express, March 30, 2003.

Rotberg, Robert, The New Nature of Nation-State Failure, http://www.twq.com/02summer/rotverg.pdf.

Schlesinger, Arthur M., A Thousand Days: John F. Kennedy in the White House, Houghton Miflin Company, 1965.

Sisk, Timothy, Power Sharing and International Mediation in Ethnic Conflicts, Washington, D.C, United States Institute of Peace, 1999.

Thomas, Clive, Trapped in a vicious circle, Stabroek News, June 1, 2003.

Thomas, Clive, Corruption in aid and political attitudes, Stabroek News, June, 8, 2003.

Woolford, Hazel, A History of Political Alliances in Guyana, 1953-1997, http://www.guyanacaribbeanpolitics.com/commentary/history_guyana1953-1997.html

NEWSPAPERS AND PERIODICALS

Daily Chronicle, August 7, 1975

Sunday Chronicle, August 10, 1975

Stabroek News, March 5, 2002

Stabroek News, April 1, 2002

Stabroek News, December 15, 2002

Stabroek News, June 1, 2003

Stabroek News, June 8, 2003

Stabroek News, April 18, 2004

Trinidad Express, August 25, 2002

Trinidad Express, March 30, 2003

Thunder, Vol. 7, No. 3, September-December, 1975

Thunder, Vol. 8, No. 3, July-September, 1976

Thunder, Vol. 17, No. 3, Third Quarter, 1985

NOTES

NOTES

NOTES

NOTES

NOTES

NOTES

NOTES